FIND YOUR FIT

DARE TO ACT ON GOD'S DESIGN FOR YOU

JANE KISE AND KEVIN JOHNSON

BETHANY HOUSE PUBLISHERS
MINNEAPOLIS, MINNESOTA 55438

Published by Bethany House Publishers
A Ministry of Bethany Fellowship International
11400 Hampshire Avenue South
Minneapolis, Minnesota 55438
www.bethanyhouse.com

Printed in the United States of America by
Bethany Press International, Minneapolis, Minnesota 55438

ISBN 0–7642–2147–7

For two great nephews,
Garrison and Nick Griffin.
May you find your fit in life
as easily as you've always fit in with us.

—J. K.

To Lyn
For constantly helping me to find my fit.

—K. J.

JANE A.G. KISE is a freelance writer and management consultant. She holds an M.B.A. from the University of Minnesota and trains people around the country on how to unlock their lives for God. She and her husband, Brian, have two children and live in Minneapolis.

KEVIN JOHNSON served as senior editor for adult nonfiction at Bethany House Publishers and pastored a cool group of more than four hundred sixth through ninth graders at Elmbrook Church in metro Milwaukee. While his training includes an M.Div. from Fuller Theological Seminary and a B.A. in English and Print Journalism from the University of Wisconsin—River Falls, his current interests include cycling, guitar, and shortwave radio. Kevin and his wife, Lyn, live in Minnesota with their three children—Nate, Karin, and Elise.

ACKNOWLEDGMENTS

Thanks to Sandra Hirsh and David Stark, who gave us free rein with the *LifeKeys* materials.

To Liz Holtman and Jan Major, two great teenagers who not only know type but gave up time in the sun on their vacations to talk with Jane about type and teens.

. . . and all the *LifeKeys* participants who cried, "Where was this when I was 16!"

BOOKS BY JANE KISE

JANE'S MANY BOOKS INCLUDE

LifeKeys
SoulTypes
Work It Out

To find out more about Jane Kise's books
visit the Web site: http://www.lifekeys.com

BOOKS BY KEVIN JOHNSON

EARLY TEEN DEVOTIONALS

Can I Be a Christian Without Being Weird?
Could Someone Wake Me Up Before I Drool on the Desk?
Does Anybody Know What Planet My Parents Are From?
So Who Says I Have to Act My Age?
Was That a Balloon or Did Your Head Just Pop?
Who Should I Listen To?
Why Can't My Life Be a Summer Vacation?
Why Is God Looking for Friends?

BOOKS FOR YOUTH

Catch the Wave!
Look Who's Toast Now!
What Do Ya Know?
What's With the Dudes at the Door?*
What's With the Mutant in the Microscope?*

To find out more about Kevin Johnson's books
visit his Web site: http://www.thewave.org

*with James White

CONTENTS

A detailed teaching guide for *Find Your Fit* is available at
www.thewave.org/fit.htm

MAKE YOUR PARENTS READ THIS!

TO THE PARENTS OF
FIND YOUR FIT READERS

Besides Jane's experience coaching adults in career transitions and Kevin's background as a youth pastor, we're both parents. Our children are still young enough that playing major league baseball is part of conversations about growing up, but we, too, are working to guide our children toward lives of meaning and fulfillment.

Find Your Fit is designed to help teens see themselves through God's eyes, maybe for the first time in their lives.

—Not how they look through the eyes of a media-crazed world that tells them, "It's how you look and shoot hoops that determines what you're worth."

—Not how they look through the eyes of school systems that tell them, "It's how you do on standardized tests and whether you shine in class discussions that determines what you're worth."

—Not how they look through the eyes of peers who tell them, "It's whether you're in the right crowd that determines what you're worth."

What teens and young adults discover in *Find Your Fit* about their value and giftedness applies both to what they might do as workers for God's kingdom and to their own career plans—which for many people are one and the same! Through the five lenses we present, teens can explore their God-given design and understand that they are valuable to God. They'll identify their

- Talents—and realize that they have *many*, even if their "Life Gifts" aren't the ones the world celebrates
- Spiritual Gifts—and recognize that God gifts people to work together for purposes bigger than themselves
- Personality Type—and understand their natural preferences for working and communicating
- Values—and build a structure for making good, godly decisions
- Passions—and begin to pattern a life of fulfillment and significance.

Why so many lenses? Because so many people find it difficult to believe that they're custom-designed for a life of meaning and purpose. We've taken people from age 15 to 90 through *LifeKeys*, the adult version of *Find Your Fit*. People arrive at self-acceptance at a variety of points in the process. If someone says, "Even if God did give me these talents, they aren't worth much," perhaps as she discovers personality type she'll exclaim, "So that's why I'm different— and I'm still normal!" Only with this kind of self-acceptance are people free to carry out the purposes God intends for them.

Entwined with the process of using our gifts for God's purposes is making career choices—and *Find Your Fit* applies to both. You can use *Find Your Fit* with your teen to help him explore schooling options or the world of work.

During many *LifeKeys* seminars, parents approach Jane with questions about their nearly-grown children:

- "Our daughter wants to join her friends at an out-of-state college when the one nearest us has a nationally-acclaimed business school. Shouldn't she do the practical thing?"
- "Our son's such a dreamer—wants to be the next George Lucas. How do we get him to be realistic?"

■ "For three generations everyone in our family has gone to college—and now this child just wants to build houses. Shouldn't we at least make him get a business degree?"

All well-meaning parents want the best for their children and want them to invest education dollars and precious post–high school years wisely. But there are no guarantees for job success these days. Even more important, we all have different definitions of success. If you truly want to help your teenagers get on the right career road— as well as a lifetime of fulfilling service to God—you can help them discover their giftedness by giving them three of the most generous, loving presents you've ever provided.

YOUR FIRST GIFT—FIND YOUR OWN FIT

Go through these exercises yourself (or use the adult version, *LifeKeys*). Even if you love your job or volunteer activities, finding your own fit will let you and your teen talk through many issues using the same vocabulary. Chances are you have different personality types. Use that information to discover how differently you approach making decisions or using your strenths. Look at each other's life gifts. In these last years together before your teen leaves home, make the most of your similarities and use your differences to talk through life choices.

Above all, if your teen's career ideas strike you as impractical or misguided, listen in silence until you have time to review your teen's "All About Me" summary at the end of the book. What about your teen's unique makeup leads him or her to these ideas? Are there ways the idea truly fits your teen? Maybe it *is* a crazy idea—or maybe the two of you are just very different. *Find Your Fit* provides a structure for working through conflicts using facts instead of opinions and emotions.

YOUR SECOND GIFT—
LET YOUR TEENAGER
EXPLORE

As much as you probably want your teenager to focus on a career so he or she chooses the right technical training or college—especially any time you contemplate that tuition price tag—too much focus too soon can block the possibility of ever finding an optimal career choice.

More than half the students who start college this year won't finish in five years. One major reason is midstream changes. Students start with an unresearched, pragmatic career choice. Along about their third semester of college they discover they have neither aptitude nor interest to pursue that choice. One of our friends was already accepted into dental school before he spent a single day observing in a dentist's office. He hated it. There he was, his senior year, without any career goals.

The goal of *Find Your Fit* is as much to *broaden* thinking about possible careers as it is to *point toward* possible fields. Your child probably knows what you do. Help your teenager explore a variety of options, especially those far-removed from your own experiences. As he or she completes *Find Your Fit*, list different occupations for first-hand research before choosing a technical school or college. Your teen will probably need your help making those connections.

YOUR THIRD GIFT—LET
THEM DREAM

Some surveys show that more than 25% of college students are business majors—yet won't necessarily have enough business skills to land a first job. That explains why a third of all pizza-delivery drivers in some areas have a college degree. And more people train as doctors and lawyers than there are positions in the medical and legal fields. What "makes sense" and seems "a sure bet to getting a job" just may not work.

If your teen's career dreams seem just that to you—impossible dreams—help shape a contingency plan. Maybe your son *will* dance with the Joffrey Ballet, but you might encourage him to get a teaching certificate in physical education. Maybe your daughter *will* be an astronaut, but logging hours toward her commercial pilot's license could be the ticket toward full employment. Help your teen discover an excellent second-best they can live with.

Talk about the realistic odds of achieving their ultimate career ambitions, but let your teen decide whether to keep on or change directions. We counsel all too many 50-year-olds who are still mourning their dream of making their lives as fishing guides or Broadway singers or politicians. In most cases someone else stomped on their dream. They never had the chance to let it go of their own accord.

We hope that *Find Your Fit* will foster meaningful and productive conversation between you and your teenager as well as impart knowledge that helps your teen take the place God designed just for him or her in the work of the kingdom. While we won't guarantee that this book will usher in a lifetime of wealth and happiness, we do believe that working to discover how God made us wisely and values us highly can bring the abundant life Jesus promised.

FIND

YOUR

FIT!

IF THE SNEAKER FITS, WEAR IT

Put yourself in the sneakers of Kevin Garnett.

You're 21. You're a third-year forward for the Minnesota Timberwolves, a swell job in pro basketball you landed straight out of high school. You're starting in the upcoming NBA All-Star Game. You're dribbling opponents' heads into the floor. And you just signed a six-year, $126 million contract.

Do the math: You've got a killer job, bushels of cash, stadiums full of friends—or at least lots of people who wish they were your friends. You're living a dream.

So what's Garnett's take on his situation? "I'm having nowhere near as much fun as I had in my first two years," he tells a reporter. "I don't know what triggers it. I think I'm being just a little too hard on myself. . . . I need to do some soul searching. I need to find myself."

WOULDN'T YOU THINK YOU HAD IT MADE?

You'd think if you were Kevin Garnett you'd be goofy with happiness. Like someone had pinched you awake in the middle of a fantastic dream—and then you discovered the dream was *real.*

It's possible to go through high school, graduate, and not be sure what you want to do with your life. In fact, it's typical. It's even possible to get to your 20s or way beyond and still feel lost. Just when you'd like to kick back and enjoy, you might feel like you've misplaced your brain. Just when you want to live your dream, you wonder if you've found it at all.

And get this news: Even if you find a dream, *happiness won't happen if your dream doesn't fit you.* No matter how good life gets on the outside, you won't be content on the inside . . .

unless you find yourself

unless you know what you want and figure out a way to chase it.

And—get this, too—

unless you figure out what God has to do with it.

Like Kevin Garnett, you need to know what your life adds up to.

Garnett might have a bunch of other gifts, but one thing is for sure: He's built to do basketball. He loves to play. He may feel like a misfit for a bit, but he'll get back at his game.

And you?

You've probably already figured out whether you care if you make the WNBA, CIA, or MIB. You probably don't plan to play pro ball, chase the baddest of the bad guys, or hunt down aliens anytime soon.

Even so, you're expected to know what you want out of life. You'll need *money.* Not Kevin Garnett's $126 million, but enough to put vittles on the table without resorting to roadside scrape-and-bake. You know you'll want *independence.* Even if you aren't ready to fly out of the house quite yet, someday it will sound like a good idea. Maybe part of you wants *adventure.* To see the world or live off the land.

Have you thought about what you want to do after work? You probably yearn for some *self-expression.* You can learn to paint watercolors, write books, or cook throat-clearing chili. Jingling somewhere in the back of your mind is probably a wish for *love.* You want friends, marriage, kids, the happily-ever-after thing. And deep down inside all of us there's a need for *spirituality.* We need to know and follow God.

Whether you think you've got a plan that will guide you well—or you're terrified of what's on the other side of school and hate to think about it—here's what makes all those things possible: *finding your fit*. You need to know who you are. And why you're here on planet Earth. And what you can do best in life.

Your *fit* affects everything. How you'll make a living. Whether you'll be able to choose a career or be forced to take whatever boring job sneaks into your life. It's part of what determines what your marriage and family will feel like. Or if you'll have the guts—if you choose—to do something wacky like waiter or waitress your way across Europe. Finding your fit even influences how you see God mattering in your life.

In other words, finding your fit couldn't be bigger.

MAKING IT COOL TO BE YOU

Once upon a time—when you were little—people let you be yourself. It was okay to be *you*. Your kindergarten teacher, for example, let you roam. You wandered from finger painting to playing store to building blocks to whamming with a hammer. On a whim you could be an artist, a business person, an architect, or a construction worker.

In first grade you had to settle down. Teachers told you to plant in one spot—your desk. Still, people did everything they could to make that spot comfortable. Big kids got big desks, small kids got small desks. If the desk didn't fit or you grew a bunch, a custodian came running with a wrench to make an adjustment. Everything was just right. You taped your name on the front, loaded in your stuff, and claimed that desk as your own. No one messed with your desk—it was *yours*. It was an extension of *you*.

Contrast that with school now. Desks come in one size. They're often first come, first served, and any assigned seat is only yours for an hour. However you're shaped, you contort to match the proportions of that desk—you do the *slouch*, the *legs crossed*, the *sit straight up*. Seven or eight hours a day you're caged. Don't even think of putting your feet up.

PLOPPING INTO GOD'S BEST

Find Your Fit is built on the view that God has made you uniquely and values you highly. While people around you may want to squeeze you into a one-size-fits-all spot, God has better plans for you. In God's plan, it's okay again to be who you are. Whether you're tall, small, wide, or narrow, God's got a desk for you. Plus drafting tables, artist's studios, computer workstations, and desk-free desks.

We're not just talking about jobs—but the grand desk of life.

God has a variety of places and purposes.

Not a single one is a cage.

And one of them is custom-built for you.

But because you're expected to conform in so many areas of life, it may not be obvious to you how God made you uniquely or how that uniqueness should affect the life you lead. To find your fit takes effort. Exploration. Discernment. *Find Your Fit* helps you do that work. It gives you tools to discover how God has gifted you in ways you've never thought of—and it tells how you can use those gifts to pursue God's best for your life. It will help you know yourself better and prime your thoughts about careers. It can lead you into areas where you can serve God and people. It will encourage you to try new things and spot special interests. Most of all, it will help you find freedom to be what God made you to be.

When God gives freedom, it's a gift unlike any other. God wired you, knows you inside and out. God's in charge of the universe but isn't an ogre out to kick you around. The Bible puts the promise to those willing to follow God like this: "For I know the plans I have for you," declares the Lord, "plans to prosper you and not to harm you, plans to give you hope and a future" (Jeremiah 29:11). When God shows you what to do, it's the absolute best for you.

BUMPER-CAR COMMANDOS

God shows you his best in a couple ways. The Bible makes loads of do's and don'ts plenty clear. Like a bumper-car rink, these clear commands set obvious boundaries of right and wrong—like "don't lie," "don't kill," "don't steal." Or, as Jesus said, "love God totally" and "love others as much as you love yourself." Drive outside of God's boundaries and your car just plain dies.

Within that bumper-car rink, though, you're free to blast around. For a while you might think it's fun to zing wildly all over the rink. But if you really want to get your job done, you figure out how to steer. To aim. To execute. Without knowing how to steer, you'll never get to the body-rattling bang-ups.

While God gives huge amounts of direction, you also have huge amounts of freedom. No Bible verse lists your name and tells you that your life will be best spent by becoming a geologist and teaching third grade Sunday school. No Scripture tells you if, where, or when to attend college or what job to take when you finish. Even so, God hasn't left you to spin circles in the bumper-car rink of life.

We believe that the best way to steer within God's boundaries is *to clue in to what God wants you to do by looking at how you're made.* Look at the rest of God's creation: Eagles soar. Dolphins leap. Cougars blaze. They're doing what they were meant to do. They're at home. They don't try to swap places. Now, you're no one-talent sloth or skunk merely good at slinking through the jungle or stinking up the woods and nothing more. You're more flexible than that. Get in a plane and you can outsoar an eagle. Hop on a Jet-Ski and you can outleap a dolphin. You and a Yugo can outrun a cougar. But you resemble these animals in this way: God made you with a unique combination of gifts to fulfill a unique role in the universe.

If your first job is to learn and stay inside the clear boundaries God put forth in the Bible, we believe your second job is to learn to function in creation as *you*.

LOOKING FOR YOURSELF IN ALL THE WRONG PLACES

Back in the sixties people were famous for gassing up their cars, drugging up their brains, and heading off on wild road trips to "find themselves." Those who didn't do a drug-induced crash-and-burn discovered only one thing: how far a vintage VW Bug could go on a tank of gas. That self-discovery strategy was stupid, but the desire behind the drive was powerful. Fact is, in the last thirty or forty years the need to know yourself has gotten stronger. The more rapidly your world changes, the closer you have to keep track of who you are.

Ponder this: If you want to find yourself, where should you look? You could learn from

- *Peers:* Good friends can tell you a lot about you. The closer they are to you, though, the less objective they might be. The further they are, well, the less they really know you. Or even like you. And whether they want to help you or harm you, peers may not be completely honest. When your peers pick the "most likely to" people for the yearbook—are they ever 100% right?
- *School:* Some schools seem happy to let you drift out the door with no direction for your future. Other schools do a lot to help you figure out who you are, using quizzes much like what you'll get in *Find Your Fit*. (Except we think ours are more fun—and our assortment perhaps better rounded!) Here's the catch to finding yourself at school: What you feed your teachers or counselors determines the accuracy of what they feed back to you. If you joke your way through aptitude tests or lie your way through personality profiles, the guidance you'll get will be badly flawed.

- *Parents:* Now you're getting warmer. Some of the exercises in *Find Your Fit* can involve your parents, because whether you admit it or not, even whether you get along fabulously or not, they often know you better than anyone else. One problem: Parents can go to extremes—they might see you as the baby who can do no wrong, or the renegade who can do no right. Ask them to talk straight with you, and try hard to hear them.

Find Your Fit is one wild way to focus in on your gifts and find out all about you. It will help you look inside at how *God* made you. This book will help you discover five crucial things about yourself: your talents, spiritual gifts, personality, values, and passions. It's like taking X-rays of your innards from five different angles.

IT ALL ADDS UP TO YOU

You may have heard the saying "God doesn't make junk." It's true. God created you and therefore values you hugely. You were made uniquely, and therefore there is truly only one of you in the world. God has good stuff in mind for you. But that saying can be thin—like cheap makeup that can't cover a whopper breakout. It's usually uttered by friends or parents to boost your self-esteem when you fail a test or can't find a date. Problem is, they often offer feeble support for their kindhearted words. In contrast, we want to help you find the *facts* about the truly important inward things that make you—oh gag, but there's no better word—*special.*

Find Your Fit offers you truth about yourself. Through quizzes, questions, examples, and stories, you'll look at yourself and examine the following:

- *Talents:* your interests—your natural bent, the assortment of things you do well.
- *Spiritual gifts:* your abilities to carry out work God wants done— the inner giftings that let you be part of purposes bigger than what you can do alone.

- *Personality types:* your built-in preferences for where you feel most comfortable—things like how you are energized, how you take in information, how you make decisions, and how you steer your life.
- *Values:* your thoughts on what is strongly important—your gut-level rankings of what is important enough to influence your decisions big and small or to cause you to take a stand.
- *Passions:* your feelings for what makes you happy—a practical guide to wrapping together the who and where of what you really love.

These five "X-rays" obviously won't show you everything about yourself. But they give great insight into what makes you *you* and what makes you different from other people. They highlight major stuff you don't usually think about but that go a long way to describe who you are. In the process you'll discover that each one of us is, as the Bible tells us, "fearfully and wonderfully made" (Psalm 139:14). Not *frightfully* made—like when you wake up and your hair wangs all over and your breath smells like hamsters slept in your mouth— but assembled according to God's awesome design.

SO WHAT'S THE CATCH?

The tools are here. God wants you to understand yourself, the purposes for your life, the gifts chosen for you from God's stockpile of ultimate wisdom and ultimate love. So what would keep you from finding your fit? *You.* Here's why:

- You might feel *rushed: "Who has time for that?"* You may feel a push to get a job—to beat your peers into the workplace. But you have a lifetime to spend. You don't want to join the millions of people who ditched thorough training of whatever sort and shortchanged their own development.
- You might feel *spiritual: "God says I'm supposed to 'lose myself'— I just want to focus on Jesus."* Look at this process as a way to

figure out what you and you alone have to offer to Jesus. Kevin admits, for example, to not exploring all of his options as a high schooler because of a drive to enter ministry. Fortunately, he still feels he found where he functions best. That doesn't always happen.

■ You might feel *slammed: "I don't have the right gift. I don't like what I find—no one else likes me, so why would I?"* You may play the bassoon better than anyone else in your school—because no one else plays it. It's a bizarre talent, a little like putting a straw up your nose and making a tune. But don't knock it. It got one friend of ours a full-ride scholarship to a top university, followed by a full-time job in a symphony.

■ You might feel *scared: "I'm not any good at anything."* If you want to be yourself, you first have to know yourself. Amy VanDyken—the first U.S. woman to win four gold medals at one Olympics—was a wretched swimmer early in high school. But she persevered. She rolled together natural talent, coaches' directions, and a desire to go for gold.

■ You might feel *overwhelmed: "I don't want to work that hard."* You could be the bestest basketball player ever, with scads of scouts recognizing your potential and big schools inviting you to study for free. Does that mean you just sit down at center court and wait for the offers to roll in? Nope. You can't identify your giftings and expect them to carry you. *You* hit the gym. *You* practice. *You* work out.

■ You might feel *smug: "I don't need to think about that now."* True, a lot of what's in this book is about your future. It's also about now—what paths you're laying out for yourself. You can ignore how you're wired. But don't be surprised if someday you've become just another nameless kid who grew up to do whatever other people told you to do.

The catch in *Find Your Fit* is that *you* have to do the work, though we do promise you'll have fun doing it. After all, you're the only person who lives inside your skin twenty-four hours a day. You're the only one with years of experience being you.

So if you're ready, plunge ahead. Take the exercises seriously. Try hard to hear God's heart of love for you in what we say. And go ahead and unwrap God's gifts to you.

ONE LAST THING
BEFORE YOU START

We want one more chance to help you start off *Find Your Fit* looking inside yourself in the right way—the way God sees you. Two humongous hints:

1. ERASE ALL OLD MESSAGES.

Everyone hears *wrong* messages, and if you take the wrong ones to heart you may never find your gifts.

Maybe you had an art teacher who said, "*Grapes* are purple, the *vines* are green. Don't you know that?" Lucky they weren't around when Monet started painting or he might have given up, too.

Case in point? Jane and Kevin each took one—count one—creative writing course in their school careers. Both were made to feel utterly unimaginative and uninspired. If we could remember those teachers' names—mercifully drowned by the healing waves of time— we'd publish them right here with a big, unChristian "Nyah nyah nyah."

Instead, we'll just ask you to revisit similar messages you may have received. "Oh, you're a clod." "You're stupid." "If you can't do those simple division problems, forget about algebra or calculus." "You don't have the patience to do a research project." Get a second opinion—from God.

2. BE BRAVE ENOUGH TO BE YOURSELF.

If you're doing *Find Your Fit* with friends or at church or in any sort of group, don't be afraid to be the only one who admits to having a certain area of interest. Or personality preference. Or career interest. This isn't a popularity contest. No adult gets to be Homecoming Queen as a long-term career.

If you're uncomfortable being a loner—don't give up. Be true to your interests, follow that path to a career—and *abracadabra!* You'll be surrounded by people like you. People who followed similar paths because you have things in common. The alternative? Hiding from yourself and trying to fit into places made for someone else.

Okay? Repeat after us:

"I'm going to like what I discover about myself
because I know that God has a plan in mind for me"

and turn the page. You're ready to begin.

FIND

YOUR

FIT!

HOW TO LOCATE A LIFE: TALENTS

If you're a wolf, how you spend your life all depends on where you're born. Minnesota wolves hang out in the forest and eat deer, while Alaska wolves live on the tundra and dine on mice. No choice in occupation. Or diet. No broad range of talents, either, from boy wolf to girl wolf. All wolves run, jump, track, and bite, some just a bit better than others. A wolf doesn't pause to ponder how happy he is about his fate. He just *does*—driven by instinct, corraled by environment.

But you're a *homo sapien*. You have choices.

Unlike wolves, humans have different talents. You got a whole bunch installed by God before you were born. Besides that, your environment is expanding. Your whole world is changing, churning out new ideas and new opportunities by the microsecond. On top of that, *you* are growing. Each day—if you spend it well—gives you new skills, new wisdom, new resources to follow God into new things.

You can do the human equivalent of moving north and eating mice, or heading south and dining on deer. Your world gives you a chance to choose—different places to live, work, who to hang out with. Distinctly diverse futures.

SMILEY FACES AND LAST PICKS

Problem is, by the ripe old age of nine or so, you probably stuck yourself with one of three labels:

- *"I've got it all."* You know you're smart, athletic, attractive. You make friends easily. You got a string of smiley faces on your papers in kindergarten, and since then you've figured there's nothing you can't do.
- *"I lost out."* Somehow you've gotten the message that life isn't kind. Maybe you draw art even your mother doesn't love. Maybe you struggle at school, or maybe you've been the last kid chosen for any team you've ever been on.
- *"I don't want to think about it."* Some days are good, some not so great. You feel absolutely average. You have no grand dreams and no freeze-action phobias, so you ignore how you might fit into the future.

Any of these ways of looking at yourself—puffing up or blowing off your talents, or ignoring them altogether—misses the truth about you. Thinking you can be anything you want—that's an unreal fantasy. Feeling you're as worthwhile to the world as a clump of sod— that's a dirty lie. Indefinitely delaying thinking about you—that's just not a good idea because you'll waste your life and miss out on all the fun.

Parents carry pictures of their kids in their wallets. You carry a picture of yourself in your brain. Unfortunately, whatever picture you carry—can we be blunt?—you don't see yourself with total accuracy. You don't see the ultimate coolness of you the way God sees it. And as you pegged yourself as good-at-everything, bad-to-the-bone, or forever-stuck-in-the-middle, you were probably missing one crucial piece of information: *God made you with a purpose in mind.* Look at what Ephesians 2:10 says about why God made you:

For we are what [God] has made us, created in Christ Jesus for

good works, which God prepared beforehand to be our way of
life. (NRSV)

God designed you to do good stuff. To accomplish something. *And*
God's given you the talent it takes.

YOU DESERVE A BREAK TODAY

Do you doubt that God could have fantabulous plans for you?

It all hangs on whether you recognize the gifts God has built into
you.

You'll have a hard time seeing your own gifts if you're blinded
by the blaze of highly visible talents. People cheer for Olympic med-
allists, big money-makers, and Nobel Prize winners. And that's likely
to make you think whatever gifts *you* have aren't any big deal. Face
it: If you aren't a Tara Lipinski winning Olympic gold at 15—or the
Hanson brothers happily producing a hit rock video by the ages of
11, 14, and 17—it might not seem obvious to you or anyone else
that you're talented.

Talents are more than being able to survive a piano recital without biffing or being able to lick the tip of your nose with your
tongue. They're broader than that. The talents we're talking about
are so big you can think of them as "life gifts," a wild variety of things
you can be good at. God's interest isn't limited to people who can
jam on ice or *MMMbop* the planet. Despite the way some talents daz-
zle, the world really doesn't revolve around figure skaters or pop
stars. Whatever life gifts you have, they're part of God's design to
keep this planet spinning. They aren't second best. Think about
some of your everyday actions—talents, really—that could bring a
"Yahoo!" from God:

- Do friends come to you with their problems? If they know you'll
  listen well, that's a talent. Not everyone knows how to hear
  people.

- Can you rescue a teacher when the VCR just won't start? Or set up a portable projector blindfolded? Not everyone has technical prowess.
- Is your bedroom fit to film a commercial for *Good Housekeeping* even if your allowance doesn't depend on it? Not everyone has a knack for organization.

You might have dozens of gifts like these—talents that won't get you a spot on Leno or Letterman, but that will let you take your place in God's show. So how could you have missed them?

WARNING: HIDDEN TREASURES AHEAD

Talents can stay buried for a long time because you don't look for them. Or you downplay them. Or don't recognize them as gifts.

There's another huge reason you might not have found your unique talents until now. You probably haven't had all that many choices in the activities you pursue. At school, for example, you and everyone else takes pretty much the same basic classes. You might get to choose whether you take business math or advanced trig, but most of your schedule is carved in stone.

Or think about how you spend your free time—lessons, hobbies, sports, extracurricular activities. How did you choose those? By what your friends did? By picking from what was offered after school or at a nearby park? Because your mom or dad prodded you? Chances are you saw only a few possibilities compared to all of what is out there.

Once you hit college or tech school, though, your choices expand. After you clobber the core courses everybody takes, you study what you want. You get a huge smorgasbord of schedules and teachers and subjects.

And in the world of work, your choices explode. There are thousands of jobs you don't even know exist. To top it all off, there are some truly significant things you can do that you might not get paid for. Not to mention new interests to search out and stuff to do just for fun. If you're going to be smart in how you choose between all these options, you've got to understand how you're wired.

DECODING YOUR BRAIN

Price scanners decode what looks like a random bunch of lines to pull up all sorts of information about a product. You may feel as indecipherable as those little stripes of black-and-white. Believe it or don't, however, there *is* order in how you're put together. And the right type of decoder can tell you a lot about you.

For decades, people have used a theory of "interest areas" in the world of work[1] to find their fit. Why? Work is where you spend a big lump of your life. (More on that later.) But it also handily clues you in to your talents. These work-based interest areas are a crucial description of what you like and what you are like.

Psychologists and others who study talents have noticed that people and their gifts cluster in six areas. They're grouped because they relish *similar tasks*—they like to do the same stuff. They enjoy *similar co-workers*—they share common interests with the people they work with. They're attracted to *similar work environments*—they like to work in groups or alone, in settings structured or loose, noisy or quiet. Here are the clusters:

- Realistic [R]
- Investigative [I]
- Artistic [A]
- Social [S]
- Enterprising [E] and
- Conventional [C].

Think of the world of work as a hexagon:

---

[1]John Holland's theory of vocational choices is the foundation for this section. His work was the basis for the *Strong Interest Inventory*™, available through your school counseling center or local community college if you want to dig deeper.

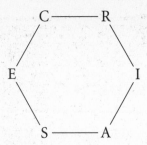

Interest areas closest to each other have the most in common—R and I, for example, are more similar than R and A. It's likely you have more than one interest area. Most people are a blend of at least two areas, generally ones next to each other. Being a blend of opposites, like R and S, is normal, too, just not as common.

Use the next pages to find out which interest areas best describe you, and then we'll go on to finding your specific talents. We start each page with a basic description of each type, then roll out a variety of characteristics that help differentiate types. See where you spot yourself, and then rejoin us on page 53.

CHECKING OUT THE INTEREST AREAS

1. Flip through the next several pages and just look at the cartoons. Which picture would you like of you in the yearbook? Choose one or two of the cartoons that fit you best and concentrate on those pages first.

2. Pull out a pen or highlighter as you read through the descriptions on the pages you chose first. What sounds like you? Have you tried any of the things described? *And* ignore what you "should" be. What are you really like?

3. When you've finished reading the descriptions for the areas you chose first, go back through and read the others, again highlighting anything that sounds like you. Once you've read through all of the descriptions, rate each interest area on how well it describes

you: (1—This interest area describes me well; 2—Parts of the description of this interest area sound like me; 3—This isn't me at all)

___ Realistic
___ Investigative
___ Conventional
___ Artistic
___ Enterprising
___ Social

Not to keep any secrets, Jane and Kevin are both SAI—writers (A) who like to help people (S) but spend hours with our heads in books (I).

4. Now you can use these interest areas to guide you in finding your talents. Turn first to the pages that describe your top interest area. Some big hints: Pretend that you don't care what your friends will think. Forget about being modest. Read the description of each life gift and ask yourself, "Is this something I like to do? Would this be fun to try if I get the chance?" Then decide whether it is one of your life gifts. Give a score from 0 to 10 based on:

0=Never done and don't want to
5=I'd like to try this *or* I've enjoyed this and think I could do it well with more experience
10=I do this all the time and love it!

You probably won't have all the life gifts in your top interest area, but chances are you'll have several of them.

5. If you come across a life gift you've never tried—like performing in a play or operating heavy machinery—think of how you've seen others using that gift. Can you picture yourself doing similar things? Does it strike you as something that would be easy or hard to learn?

6. Do the same for all of the interest areas—read through the life gift descriptions and decide which ones you have. You may have at least one in each of the interest areas, even those that don't sound

much like you. For example, Jane chokes on most Conventional tasks, but she does have a life gift for managing time and priorities.

7. Once you've searched for your talents in all 6 interest areas, go back through and highlight your *top 5–10 life gifts (talents)*. The ones you *know* are yours. The ones you most like to use. Write those on page 207.

THE REALISTIC PERSON

If you're a *Realistic* type, chances are you grew up wanting to be outside at every chance—running, climbing, jumping, enjoying nature. Your favorite toys might have included building blocks, trucks out in the sandbox, or "real" toys like workbenches, ironing boards, and lawn mowers. You may also enjoy athletics.

In school, Realistics prefer hands-on activities—constructing models rather than just reading about different habitats, for example.

You do best when teachers convince you that what you are learning is relevant.

Realistics might save money toward all kinds of tools—for hobbies, gas and insurance to ensure access to a car, camping equipment, or fees for lift tickets, fishing licenses, etc.

THINGS REALISTICS DO OR DREAM ABOUT TRYING:
- Sports
- Hunting, fishing, camping
- Whitewater rafting, bungee-jumping, rock climbing
- Training, raising animals
- Working with or operating cars, boats, planes, mowers, etc.
- Gardening

THE REALISTIC PERSON (CONTINUED)

REALISTIC HEROES:
Indiana Jones (adventurer and archaeologist who doesn't need anyone's help), Rocky (Sly Stallone as a prize-fighter), Amelia Earhart (explorer), Sally Ride (astronaut), Tim Taylor (Tim Allen as the Tool Man on *Home Improvement*).

SOMETHING REALISTICS GET IN TROUBLE FOR AT SCHOOL:
Blowing off any work you don't see as useful in "real life."

GENERALLY, REALISTICS WOULD RATHER:
- be part of the stage crew than the acting company
- solve a problem alone than work with a group
- go bowling than go to an art museum
- share your life savings than share your feelings

OTHERS MIGHT SEE REALISTICS AS:
- reliable, cool in a crisis
- apt to take physical risks
- hating to be the center of attention
- content to be alone or with just a few close friends

REALISTICS MIGHT LIKE WORK:
that lets you create results you can touch or see, uses large or fine motor skills, that allows for practical approaches to problems, and where you can focus on things rather than on people, ideas, or data.

TYPICAL REALISTIC CAREERS:
engineer, forester, race-car driver, building contractor, police officer, pilot, military officer, athletic trainer, industrial arts teacher, animal trainer.

REALISTICS MIGHT VOLUNTEER TO:
paint houses, shovel snow, provide transportation, refinish/repair furniture or machinery, lead outdoor activities.

THE REALISTIC PERSON (CONTINUED)

REALISTIC LIFE GIFTS	When have I used this? Is it fun for me? Does it feel natural? Was it easy to learn?	Score 0–10 0=Hate it 10=Love it
Mechanical aptitude—knows how things work and can understand and apply mechanics and physics		
Operating heavy equipment, driving, piloting—can handily run construction equipment or big transportation vehicles		
Manual dexterity—skilled at using hands or fine tools in woodworking, sewing, etc.		
Building mechanical/structural devices—able to design, assemble, or fix stuff		
Physical coordination—able to get large muscles all moving in the same direction—possesses the agility needed in sports, skilled trades, etc.		
Organizing supplies or implements—able to sort and store in a way that makes finding and maintaining materials easy—whether in a locker, bedroom, or warehouse		
Taking physical risks—attracted to activities or occupations that can be physically dangerous		
Emotional stability, reliability—able to react calmly to situations and stay on course		

THE INVESTIGATIVE PERSON

If you're an *Investigative* type, you probably asked "Why?" dozens of times each day growing up—if you didn't have your nose in a book or your eyes glued to a toy telescope. You might collect and classify shells, insects, or rocks or simply spend time observing ants or clouds—analyzing to figure out how things work.

In school, Investigatives often prefer science or math classes. You may even do research projects on your own—and go on to win chemistry awards. You also probably know a lot more about computers than how to stick in a floppy or type a report.

Investigatives might use allowance or earnings to buy equipment for complex hobbies like astronomy, sailing, or rock climbing. You might also upgrade your computers or stereo systems or invest in books.

THINGS INVESTIGATIVES DO OR DREAM ABOUT TRYING:
- Doing scientific or laboratory work
- Programming a computer
- Going on an archaeological dig
- Researching, theorizing, solving complex problems
- Reading scientific books and magazines
- Mastering complex hobbies—skiing, chess, etc.

THE INVESTIGATIVE PERSON (CONTINUED)

INVESTIGATIVE HEROES:
Nancy Drew, the Hardy Boys, and Sherlock Holmes (mystery-sleuths extraordinaire), Woodward and Bernstein (the reporters who broke the Watergate story), Madam Curie and Al Einstein (revolutionary scientists), Bill Nye the Science Guy (catch him on PBS).

SOMETHING INVESTIGATIVES GET IN TROUBLE FOR AT SCHOOL:
Ignoring any school subject you aren't hotly interested in so you can spend loads of time on things you like—and dissecting animals you aren't supposed to.

GENERALLY, INVESTIGATIVES WOULD RATHER:
- design your own project than do as you're told
- solve a problem alone than work with a group
- work at a library than at a retail store
- study math than give a speech

OTHERS MIGHT SEE INVESTIGATIVES AS:
- independent, self-motivated
- absorbed by their interests
- original and creative
- scholarly, intellectual

INVESTIGATIVES MIGHT LIKE WORK:
that lets you handle ideas rather than people or things, involves theory or research, and allows for independence.

TYPICAL INVESTIGATIVE CAREERS:
chemist, physician, psychologist, science teacher, pharmacist, college professor, inventor, research and development manager, systems analyst.

INVESTIGATIVES MIGHT VOLUNTEER TO:
set strategies, produce long-range plans, research background data, provide computer skills, collect or organize data, design surveys or studies.

THE INVESTIGATIVE PERSON (CONTINUED)

INVESTIGATIVE LIFE GIFTS	When have I used this? Is it fun for me? Does it feel natural? Was it easy to learn?	Score 0–10 0=Hate it 10=Love it
Inventing—able to imagine or produce useful things or theories, especially in technical or scientific areas		
Researching—good at investigating or experimenting to discover information, test theories, or find new ways to apply current knowledge		
Conceptualizing—can think up and develop abstract ideas or theories		
Working independently—able to work well without guidance or input from others		
Solving complex problems—able to solve difficult situations by using logic or data		
Computer aptitude—good at designing systems and software		
Synthesizing information—can pull together information from different sources and make it understandable		
Theorizing—can cook up explanations, find connections, or project future trends		

THE ARTISTIC PERSON

If you think way back to pre-school, *Artistic* types probably were labeled as creative, musical, artistic, dramatic—or as day-dreamers. Your favorite toys might have included arts and crafts supplies, musical instruments, props for acting, or story books and other things that allowed you to use your imagination.

In school, Artistics do best when allowed to color outside the lines and add a fresh touch to assignments. You often like to write and you do best when you like a subject and the teacher likes you. Your projects and reports may look nicer than anyone else's—though not if you thought the assignment was inane.

Artistics might use allowances or earnings to buy tickets to museums, theatres, or for books or art supplies. You might also prefer to dress originally, making a statement through what you wear.

THINGS ARTISTICS DO OR DREAM ABOUT TRYING:

- Acting or performing musically
- Painting, sculpting, photography
- Reporting for the school newspaper or radio station
- Writing poetry, stories, or novels
- Attending dance, theatre, or music concerts
- Directing videos, plays

THE ARTISTIC PERSON (CONTINUED)

ARTISTIC HEROES:
Ansel Adams (legendary photographer), Jane Austen and William Shakespeare (been paying attention in Lit class?), George Lucas and Steven Spielberg (brilliant producers), Laura Ashley (designer of everything from underwear to drapes), Bill Cosby (who even manages to make pudding funny).

SOMETHING ARTISTICS GET IN TROUBLE FOR AT SCHOOL:
Daydreaming, insisting on self-expression and uniqueness, wanting to do things your way—like producing beautiful projects that don't follow directions.

GENERALLY, ARTISTICS WOULD RATHER:
- write a story than a report
- set your own hours than follow a schedule
- go to an art museum than play cards
- take dance or music lessons than organize anything

OTHERS MIGHT SEE ARTISTICS AS:
- creative and imaginative
- nonconformist, free-spirited
- expressive, sensitive
- unstructured, flexible

ARTISTICS MIGHT LIKE WORK:
in unstructured environments where you can choose your own hours, maybe working alone or with one or two others. You might gravitate toward less businesslike environments: museums, libraries, law firms, or advertising agencies.

TYPICAL ARTISTIC CAREERS:
advertising executive, attorney, librarian, musician, reporter, broadcaster, minister, photographer, artist, public relations director.

ARTISTICS MIGHT VOLUNTEER TO:
be on a drama team, share musical or artistic talents, take part in one-time creative efforts, design and make decorations or publicity.

THE ARTISTIC PERSON (CONTINUED)

ARTISTIC LIFE GIFTS	When have I used this? Is it fun for me? Does it feel natural? Was it easy to learn?	Score 0–10 0=Hate it 10=Love it
Acting—can relate emotions or portray a character through performance, either on stage or in real life		
Writing, reporting, technical writing—can communicate clearly through writing, including reports, letters, and publications		
Verbal/linguistics skills—adept at learning languages, using and comprehending spoken words		
Musical expression—able to compose or perform music with voice, body, or instruments		
Creative problem solving—able to find unusual solutions to tough issues, especially in artistic forms or in relationships		
Sculpting/photography/ graphic arts/painting—uses art as a means to expression		
Creative design through use of space—able to work with spatial concepts, like in interior design or architecture		
Creative expression through color—able to coordinate colors and patterns, such as in clothing design, decorating, etc.		

THE SOCIAL PERSON

Growing up, *Social* types are friends with everyone—you have natural people skills. You often liked playing "School" and "House," where you could practice teaching and caring for others. You also like games that allow for socializing and forming clubs, especially if you can include everyone.

Socials look forward to school because of the friendships you develop. You tend to prefer group learning activities and enjoy working cooperatively. You want to pass on to others what you have learned. You might prefer classes like English and social studies to more scientific subjects.

Socials might use allowances or earnings for extracurricular activities, going out with friends, hobbies that let you be with others, and "self-discovery" classes.

THINGS SOCIALS DO OR DREAM ABOUT TRYING:

- Organizing parties, social events
- Traveling with friends
- Volunteer work, religious activities
- Being a foreign exchange student—or hosting one
- Working with younger children
- Developing and maintaining relationships

THE SOCIAL PERSON (CONTINUED)

SOCIAL HEROES:
Kofi Annan (a humanitarian and Secretary General of the United Nations), Mother Teresa (her heart for the outcast), Princess Diana (everybody's friend), Corrie ten Boom (who hid Jews in Nazi-occupied Holland and led Bible studies in concentration camps), Eric Liddel (missionary to China made famous in the classic movie *Chariots of Fire*).

SOMETHING SOCIALS GET IN TROUBLE FOR AT SCHOOL:
jabbering, passing notes, and planning parties when the teacher is talking.

GENERALLY, SOCIALS WOULD RATHER:
- work with a group than work alone
- tutor a younger child than drive a car
- help plan a party than work with numbers
- make a friend than read a book

OTHERS MIGHT SEE SOCIALS AS:
- friendly and cheerful
- concerned for the welfare of others
- kind and generous
- ready to listen, tactful

SOCIALS MIGHT LIKE WORK:
where you can serve others in environments that emphasize cooperation. You might gravitate toward organizations that help people (like hospitals, schools, churches, etc.) or to parts of businesses that focus on people (like customer service or training).

TYPICAL SOCIAL CAREERS:
elementary school teacher, social worker, park and recreation coordinator, physical therapist, nurse, counselor.

SOCIALS MIGHT VOLUNTEER TO:
organize fund-raisers, provide child care, plan social events, peer counseling, tutoring, lead small groups, provide hospitality.

THE SOCIAL PERSON (CONTINUED)

SOCIAL LIFE GIFTS	When have I used this? Is it fun for me? Does it feel natural? Was it easy to learn?	Score 0–10 0=Hate it 10=Love it
Teaching—knows how to instruct, demonstrate, train, or guide others in learning facts or concepts		
Listening and facilitating—able to encourage others to volunteer information and discuss issues or topics, either one-on-one or in groups		
Understanding or counseling others—able to give advice and guidance that fits the needs of others		
Conversing/informing—offers hospitality, talking and listening informally one-on-one or in small groups about daily events, issues, or personal concerns		
Being of service—considers and acts to help others		
Evaluating people's character—can spot the motives and values of other people		
Being empathetic and tactful—good at noticing how others feel and acting accordingly		
Working with others—able to establish good working relationships based on trust and respect		

THE ENTERPRISING PERSON

Once again, think way back to preschool. *Enterprising* types were the natural-born leaders, ready to take charge. You may enjoy competitive sports, figuring out how to turn everything from baseball cards to Beanie Babies into cold cash, or convincing your brothers and sisters to do your chores for you.

In school, Enterprisers may spend a lot of time figuring out how to beat the system or get elected class president. If you're on a sports team, it will be a prestigious one and you'd like to be captain. You can sell anything from wrapping paper to cheese logs and argue effectively with every teacher in the building.

Enterprising types might use earnings for the latest and greatest clothes, tickets to the biggest concerts, or any of the finer things in life.

THINGS ENTERPRISERS DO OR DREAM ABOUT TRYING:
- Being president—preferably of the country
- Partying with the "in" crowd
- Debating, giving speeches, persuading others
- Running a business
- Vacationing at expensive places
- Belonging to prestigious clubs, fraternities, or sororities

THE ENTERPRISING PERSON (CONTINUED)

ENTERPRISING HEROES:
Bill Gates (he wants to own your life), Billy Graham (who tells and sells people on God), Mary Kay (the pink Cadillac lady), Mrs. Fields (the cookiemeister), Margaret Thatcher (government is just her cup of tea).

SOMETHING ENTERPRISERS GET IN TROUBLE FOR AT SCHOOL:
scheming your way through school—sweet-talking others into doing all the work on group projects, scamming the principal out of his sweet parking spot, selling candy during study hall.

GENERALLY, ENTERPRISERS WOULD RATHER:
- lead than follow
- give a talk than write a report
- study politics than study biology
- compete and debate than research anything too deeply

OTHERS MIGHT SEE ENTERPRISERS AS:
- ambitious, adventuresome
- witty, talkative
- optimistic and full of energy
- impressed with status and possessions

ENTERPRISERS MIGHT LIKE WORK:
that is goal oriented, where you can measure success, interact with others, head up your own endeavors, and spend at least some time in the limelight.

TYPICAL ENTERPRISING CAREERS:
sales, management, marketing, personnel director, lobbyist, financial planner, TV announcer, urban planner, politician.

ENTERPRISERS MIGHT VOLUNTEER TO:
take leadership roles, spearhead evangelistic efforts, recruit others, give speeches, promote.

THE ENTERPRISING PERSON (CONTINUED)

ENTERPRISER LIFE GIFTS	When have I used this? Is it fun for me? Does it feel natural? Was it easy to learn?	Score 0–10 0=Hate it 10=Love it
Public speaking—can communicate clearly in front of a live audience		
Selling—able to convince others to purchase products or services		
Persuading—skilled at getting others to accept an idea, value, or point of view		
Leadership—able to get others to work together and direct people's efforts toward common goals		
Management—can plan, organize, and direct projects and resources to reach goals		
Negotiating—able to help others listen to the opinions or demands of others and reach agreement or compromise		
Taking action—able to respond decisively in emergency or stressful situations		
Adventurousness—willing to take above-average financial and interpersonal risks		

THE CONVENTIONAL PERSON

If you're a *Conventional* type, you probably seldom got into trouble growing up—you kept your room clean, finished your chores, and never lost the pieces to your games and puzzles. Your favorite toys might have included dolls, model trains, and games with set rules.

In school, Conventionals like subjects where success comes from mastering a set of rules, such as spelling and math, preferring topics with concrete answers to those with heavy use of theory or creativity. You often enjoy scouting and other organizations as well as community-sponsored sports leagues.

Conventionals might not spend much money. You may actually be saving for college, or for a big-ticket item like a first car. You may be quite organized about earning money—developing regular customers for lawn-mowing or baby-sitting.

THINGS CONVENTIONALS DO OR DREAM ABOUT TRYING:

- Collecting anything and everything
- Organizing belongings, supplies
- Sightseeing, visiting popular historic or amusement sites
- Building models—from rockets to doll houses
- Crossword puzzles, structured games
- Owning a cabin or vacationing at the same resort each year

THE CONVENTIONAL PERSON (CONTINUED)

CONVENTIONAL HEROES:
Margaret Hamma (world's fastest typist—according to Guinness), H & R Block (the people who help the rest of the country file their taxes), Mister Rogers (who always wears the same sweater), Miss Manners (who never uses the wrong fork), Cal Ripken, Jr. (baseball's most dependable player), Jack Wheeler (youngest Eagle Scout ever at age 12).

SOMETHING CONVENTIONALS GET IN TROUBLE FOR AT SCHOOL:
Conventionals don't get in trouble unless it's for telling on kids getting into trouble. You turn your work in on time. You're usually the one who asks, "Is this going to be on the test?" (a question the rest of us love you for).

GENERALLY, CONVENTIONALS WOULD RATHER:
- be efficient and accurate than creative
- adhere to a schedule than go with the flow
- keep club records than organize social activities
- go to a movie than act in a play

OTHERS MIGHT SEE CONVENTIONALS AS:
- neat, accurate
- pragmatic
- methodical
- contained and contented

CONVENTIONALS MIGHT LIKE WORK:
in areas that emphasize accuracy and care with details. You may prefer set schedules where you can predict what your days will be like and enjoy establishing routines.

TYPICAL CONVENTIONAL CAREERS:
accountant, banker, office manager, small business owner, business education teacher, nursing home administrator, production manager, mathematics teacher.

CONVENTIONALS MIGHT VOLUNTEER TO:
keep records, perform office tasks, organize supplies and equipment, establish procedures, accounting/auditing.

THE CONVENTIONAL PERSON (CONTINUED)

CONVENTIONAL LIFE GIFTS	When have I used this? Is it fun for me? Does it feel natural? Was it easy to learn?	Score 0–10 0=Hate it 10=Love it
Organizing—able to arrange data, money, study schedules, assembly lines, homes, etc., in a structured way		
Appraising/evaluating—able to accurately estimate the value or significance of things ranging from investments, antiques, and real estate to business opportunities, etc.		
Attending to detail—aware of pieces that make up the whole, as in printed words, administrative tasks, or the environment		
Managing time, setting priorities—good at arranging activities and schedules to consistently meet deadlines, appointments, and goals		
Calculating and mathematical skills—adept at working with numbers and figures; adding, subtracting, multiplying, dividing		
Systematizing—able to sort information or things for ease of use		
Persistence—good at follow-through and patience in handling responsibilities		
Stewardship—known for conservative handling of money, data, things, and people		

SO WHAT GOOD ARE LIFE GIFTS?

So why is it important to know your talents, or what can be called "life gifts"?

Knowing your life gifts preps you to make the most of your free time. You know about plenty of sports and hobbies. But take a trip to the magazine section of a big bookstore like Barnes & Noble to see how many utterly different ways there are to spend your non-school hours. Awareness of your life gifts shows you what you like and why—and identifies related interests you may want to try.

Knowing your life gifts clues you in to how God wants to use you in this world. Your life gifts hint at what ministry you'd be good at. Why, for example, do some people live to tell others about their faith in God? We'll see later that there is a *spiritual gift* of evangelism, but evangelists often have the life gift of being Enterprising. Would you rather be in a drama? You're probably an Artistic. Would you just as soon stay off stage and pass out bulletins and take the offering? You might be a Conventional.

Knowing your life gifts helps you like yourself for who you are. It might even rescue you from nerdhood. Ryan—a Realistic—was a shy, scrawny kid who built in the rafters of his garage the coolest fort in the neighborhood. His power-tool prowess made him a natural to head up set construction for his high school's lavish musicals. His stage crew experience earned him the nickname "Stanley"—as in the tool company—and led to a job at the Guthrie, one of the country's premiere theatres. The knowledge of hydraulics he learned working backstage teamed up with a good education to take him into the medical technology field. At his tenth high school reunion he was happy with himself and his work—and he had transmogrified into a sweet guy swinging a loving wife on his arm.

But here's the big "so what?" *Knowing your life gifts can help you find your fit in the world of work.* No single test or source of infor-mation can scream "Go be a fireman" or "You should start your own business," but knowing you're Realistic or Enterprising alerts you to the likelihood you'd do well in those fields.

JAZZING UP YOUR JOB

The goal of *Find Your Fit* isn't to push careers or rush you into premature decisions. Our intent is just the opposite—to let you explore all your options and understand why you likely would enjoy some jobs more than others.

TRUTH #1: BIG SATISFACTION COMES FROM DOING WHAT GOD MADE YOU TO DO.

TRUTH #2: IN THE ADULT WORLD THAT MEANS FINDING A JOB THAT FITS YOU.

Why is the job thing so crucial?

In just a few years, you will enter The Working Zone. Of the 168 hours in your week, you will spend

- 60 hours at work, including commute time (more in New York)
- 54 hours sleeping (six on weeknights, twelve on the weekend)
- 21 hours eating (more if you wash dishes)
- 10 hours cleaning (washing clothes, cars, etc.)
- 10 hours running errands (calling Mom, etc.)

That leaves about 13 hours a week to do what you want to do, unless . . . *Your work is something you want to do!* If you just "get a job," something that pays the bills and finances a big-screen TV, you have less than 2 hours of free time a day. If you *want* to go to work, suddenly half of your waking week is fun.

Right now you may feel like school is a prison. You do your time, but you live for afterschool activities and weekends. It would be great to fix that, but it may not be possible—for now, that is.

But consider this: Finding work that's actually fun can happen—

and the fun doesn't depend on the size of the paycheck. Look at the adults around you. Which ones can't wait to get back to their desks? And which ones hate Monday mornings? Lots of people hate work—and it's no coincidence that the most heart attacks happen at around 8 A.M. on Mondays! But people who like what they do say they find it *interesting*, find meaning in its *bigger purpose*, or find they *do it well*. Really happy people find all three are true. They make a living. Find fulfillment. Better their world. Adult fun is finding work that aligns with the way God made you.

MAKING WORK YOUR PLAYGROUND

We aren't cracking the whip to make you responsible. We're telling you that what you do for laughs can be what you do for a living. Sound good?

Exactly what you do with a life gift depends on your aptitude (your raw abilities) and achievement (what you accomplish with those abilities). It depends on how hard you work and on what you decide is important to you.

Moreover, what you want to do has to react with reality. You have to weigh, for example, whether you want to be one of the 800 violin majors (no joke!) who vie for each spot in a professional symphony. Things you'd enjoy as a vocation (your means of making a living) may need to become your avocation (a hobby that may or may not make money). You might choose a different venue for your talent. Lots of those violin majors, for example, spice up church services or have great fun teaching kids to play.

There are thousands of careers out there, but there are some fast ways to narrow down your possibilities.

First, let's get rid of what you can't do. You can't be *anything* you want to be. Yes, in many countries you have free access to any career, but if you flunked a physics test because you don't know what a ball bearing is, you can cross engineering off your list. If you're allergic to cats mentally and physically, you're not going to be a veterinarian. And if listening to people's problems annoys you, don't be a psychiatrist.

Second, you can't choose a career just for the money. Or prestige. Or power. When you're 20 and full of energy, you can probably get good enough grades to jump-start a career even if the classwork is dull. But turn the clock ahead 20 years. Now you're middle-aged, probably with a mortgage, family, and loads of grown-up responsibilities you'd never expected sapping your strength. Try sitting at your desk doing something that makes your most boring subject in school seem incredibly fascinating. Not only that, but chances are that the person in the office next door *loves* the same job and does it at least as well as you without half the effort. Adults have a word for what happens to you as you sit and wonder why work is so hard: burnout.

But you *can* start tuning in to your own design. You can forget what everyone else is doing and take some chances. After all, if you never pick up a power saw, how will you ever find out if you're cut out to work with wood? If you never give classes like English, social studies, or biology an honest chance, how will you ever know you weren't built to excel or at least do well in those areas?

Third, you can't choose a career when you're 16. The key is finding the *range* of occupations that might fit, not choosing one now only to find out later that you didn't know enough about it. You want to head in the right direction—college, vo-tech, on-the-job training. Pick the right type of school—business, service industry, liberal arts, engineering.

Ask your parents and teachers if they are doing what they wanted to be when they were 10 or 15 or even 20 years old. When Jane was a college freshman, 22 of the 24 women (not Jane) on her dorm floor said, "I'm going to be a doctor" at their first meeting. Guess what? The group produced exactly one M.D. Someone who knows from a young age what he or she wants to do for life is the exception, not the rule. Another example: When Kevin was in junior high and his mom had cancer, he decided he wanted to be a biochemist. He had great biology and chemistry teachers, fed treated sewage to mice and weighed the results, and got hired as a lab tech when he was only 17. It wasn't until college that he figured out that the precision and repetition of the laboratory bored him silly.

SO WHERE DO YOU GO FROM HERE?

As busy as you are right now, life only gets more hectic. That means *right now* is your time to explore areas that might interest you. That process of exploration is your best chance to test what you've learned about yourself and your talents.

1. *Sample classes.* Scope out the subject matter as well as the people who do well in a class—and actually enjoy the studying it takes to do well. If you're still in high school, check out community colleges and organizations for offerings. Be honest about the obvious: Which school classes so far have you liked the most—other than that American history class where you could catch up on sleep or the chemistry class where you had the cute lab partner?

2. *Do different jobs.* If you have any choice about part-time work, go for exposure to different fields before money. In other words, if you can make $12 an hour waitressing or $6 an hour working as an orderly at a nursing home—well, you have to make your own choice. But make part-time jobs count. Don't waste your summers.

3. *Volunteer.* This is a great way to test out whether you really have a certain life gift and—great news—churches have very low entry requirements. They'll let you try almost anything at least once. If you can, find someone you trust to observe you and give honest feedback.

4. *Spend a day with professionals.* Prepare questions beforehand so you know what you want to learn—nothing worse than wasting someone's workday. What did they want to be when they were little? What might you do right now to gain experience? What's the best

part of the job? What's the worst part? (By the way, catching your interviewee on a bad day will make any job sound unappealing.)

5. *Explore schools that excel in areas that might interest you.* You may not have the money, grades, or interest to attend top schools, but shoot high. Send for catalogs and see what the best schools offer so you can tailor your program wherever you go. Whatever kind of training you want to pursue, comparison shop. Visit several schools.

6. *Visit your school counselor.* He or she can provide you with an index of jobs. What you see now might not be relevant by the time you graduate, or hit your 20s and 30s or beyond. Think *fields* that fit your life gifts.

7. *Check out the resources at your local library.* You'll find that some of the work has already been done for you. Go to the call number 331 area both in the reference and open-shelf section (or just tell the librarian you're trying to find out about jobs). There are tons of books, but they are *not* light reading. Find a friend to join you. Bring some M&M's (concealed in a brown paper bag), a pad of paper, and some patience (after all, you can't visit every business you might work for even in a lifetime). Some great places to start are

- *Occupational Outlook Handbook* (U.S. Department of Labor). This volume describes 250 occupations that cover 6 out of 7 jobs available today. Learn about working conditions, earnings, employment outlook, and where to get more information.
- *Selected Characteristics of Occupations Defined in the Revised Dictionary of Occupational Titles* (U.S. Department of Labor). If you don't choke on the title, you'll find thousands of jobs described—from cocoa-bean roaster to pediatrician. Check out skills needed—compare to your life gifts!—physical demands, years of schooling required. And you can choose an interest category—like craft arts or sports—and see all the jobs listed. (Just an example: Craft arts included engravers, picture framers, fiberglass model makers, sign painters, and a whole lot of others you've never heard of.)

- *Enhanced Guide for Occupational Exploration* (JIST Works, Inc.). A book that gives data for 2,800 jobs. Find out the aptitudes you need, physical requirements to meet, employment outlook, clues about whether you'd like the work, and tips on preparing yourself for the job.

Most libraries also have pamphlet files on different vocations—a paradise for Investigatives. . . .

8. *Develop some general ideas of what careers fit you—or definitely don't fit you.* Take notes from people already in these jobs of what is essential to them. Examples might be

- *Sales:* You'd better like people—and be able to handle rejection.
- *Financial Brokerage:* You'd better be interested in multiplying money (and cool under pressure when million-dollar deals go bust).
- *Pilot:* Settle into the calm of a check-and-recheck routine—and ponder if you want to be the first to die in a crash (after all, planes don't back into mountains).
- *Accounting:* You'll love it if you love numbers—and start now saving up sleep for the crazy hours you'll likely work during tax season.
- *Teaching:* You gotta have a love for people—because teaching even at the college level offers surprisingly little time to hole up in the library alone with a stack of books.

9. *Be fearless.* The God who designed you knows how to get you to the finish line. The moral? Instead of paralyzing yourself with the fear that you'll pick the wrong route, start drawing a map. There are lots of possible roads that end up at the same destination—just make sure you get on one that's going in the right direction for *you*.

FIND

YOUR

FIT!

FITTING IN WITH GOD'S WORK: SPIRITUAL GIFTS

Picture a Christmas tree all decked out in your home—a tree with one problem: Three weeks after Christmas, needles cover the still-wrapped presents stacked underneath. Sound stupid? Who'd be dumb enough not to open those packages?

That slowness to rip through the wrapping, however, is how too many Christians approach what the Bible calls "spiritual gifts," those special abilities we receive to carry out God's purposes.

Spiritual gifts all help us build God's kingdom of love and fulfill God's plan for the world. But they come in a variety of shapes and sizes. God gives us gifts like *evangelism:* sharing faith in a way people find inviting. Or *encouragement:* comforting others who feel abandoned or hopeless. Or *teaching:* revealing God's Word so that others figure it out.

The Bible contains several lists of spiritual gifts—check out 1 Corinthians 12:1–31 and 14:1–30; Romans 12:4–8; and Ephesians 4:11–13—and many Bible students think those long and varied lists might only be samples of ways God gifts people. To keep this introduction to spiritual gifts straightforward, however, we're grouping gifts. To help you understand the main types of giftings without getting bogged down in descriptive detail, we'll look at Evangelism, Helps, Leadership, Discernment/Prophecy, Encouragement/ Mercy, Faith, Hospitality, Giving, Teaching/Wisdom/Knowledge, and Healing/Miracles/Tongues.

ROTTING BUT NOT ROTTEN

So why do Christians let these gifts rot under the tree, unwrapped and unused? Most likely because we're afraid to look inside. For five reasons:

1. *We don't know the gifts exist.* Maybe they're under a tree in a room we never enter—we think it's so holy it's off limits. While God intends people to get going and growing in gifts as soon as they join the faith race, we don't always grasp that. We figure God waits until we know everything about faith before splattering us with grace. Not so.

2. *We fear we'll hate what we receive.* Just like with life gifts, we panic that our gifts will be something less than God's best for us. Rest assured, God has better taste in gifts than your color-blind aunt who gives you itchy sweaters every Christmas.

3. *We're afraid God will ask us to use our gifts.* Deep down, most of us fear that slipped into the package with our spiritual gift will be marching orders to make haste to Ukarumpa—that's in Papau New Guinea—as a missionary. Or to make friends with a sworn enemy. We think God will require us to do something we'd rather not do. Well, maybe. But again, that's all up to God, the Giftgiver who knows us better than we know ourselves and who came to give us abundant life.

4. *We may think we're too young.* Tell that to Jesus, who taught in the temple at 12, or Timothy, who pastored a church at 16. God, of course, knows when we're ready for those kind of assignments. But God stands ready to use willing hearts of any age.

5. *We may be confused by controversy.* Some Christians argue—a lot—about which gifts God gives today. Some feel strongly that long ago God stopped passing out supernatural gifts—healing, miracles, tongues. That infighting can scare people off from discovering and using even uncontroversial gifts. *Find Your Fit* talks about possibilities, about the range of gifts you *might* have. Most gifts are no-

brainers no one discounts. Don't sweat if supernatural gifts do or don't show up in your life. Check at your church and you'll probably hear that when all the arguing cools down, most Christians agree that how and where gifts appear is ultimately *God's* choice. And those gifts let us be part of God's plan.

VOYAGE INTO THE MIND OF GOD

Get into the mind of God for a moment. You love these crazy humans so much that you sent your Son, even knowing the cost in advance, so your kind kingdom could come on this earth. Kingdom-building is a huge task, one at which people fail miserably on their own. So after Jesus' job was done, you sent the Holy Spirit to live in each person who wants to join your work. Through the Spirit, these people can take action. They can build the Church. Get others to follow God. Tell the world about Jesus. Change the minds of rulers and kings. Pull off miracles. Boldly go where no holy person has gone before. You empower people with practical tools that help the world hear about Jesus, receive him, and follow him.

Those are spiritual gifts in action.

The sad truth is that most people don't understand these gifts or know which ones they have. Only one out of five adults in the U.S. can correctly identify one of their gifts.[1] If you ask them what gifts they have, many name things that aren't spiritual gifts at all, such as friendliness, patience, being in good health, or having a sense of humor. Those are all good things, but not what we're talking about.

Yet the Bible promises us that once we join the body of Christ, we have spiritual gifts: "Now to each one the manifestation [revelation, unveiling, evidence, demonstration, gift] of the Spirit is given for the common good" (1 Corinthians 12:7, our amplification). If you're a believer, you've got 'em. You may have a gift you don't know about. And your gifts aren't like sweepstakes prizes—they really exist.

---

[1] News Release, Barna Research Group, Ltd., October 3, 1995.

GOD'S DOUBLE DARE

Pay attention to two messages here:

First, *dare to believe you have a spiritual gift*. Paul tells us that "each one" has a gift. Not just the biggie leaders. Not just the long-winded teachers. Not just the kid who wins the prize for best explaining "What God Did in My Life This Week" at the closing campfire of Bible camp. Or the one who prays like King David. God doesn't put a warning on the gifts that says, "For use only by professionals. Don't try this at home."

So since you have a spiritual gift, does that mean you're destined—or doomed, depending on how you look at it—to be a pastor or something?

Nope. There's a huge difference in where and how Christians use their gifts. Think of this distinction: There are *formal* and *informal* ministries. You can do a formal ministry like teaching Sunday school, or an informal ministry of teaching kids in the neighborhood. You can be part of a formal evangelistic team that goes to parks or malls, or informally tell peers at school about Jesus. Informal doesn't mean less intense. It means less top-down, less organized by the Church. Paid jobs like pastoring are the ultimate in formal ministry. God doesn't call many to that role. Instead, most of us are sent out to be willing workers in the midst of our everyday lives.

Second, *dare to use that gift*. God gives us gifts for "the common good." Not to make us feel great or important, but because there's an awful lot of work to be done. After all, the task of carrying out God's work hasn't gotten any easier in the last 2,000 years. Even though the number of workers has grown from 12 disciples to many millions, the earth's population grew from a couple hundred million to over 6 billion. It only takes a few minutes watching the evening news to realize that the world doesn't look much like the kingdom of God. Besides that, technology and the illusion of Christian superstars mask how necessary we are to God's plan. God still needs all of us who are willing to use our spiritual gifts.

Your spiritual gifts may look a lot like life gifts. The difference isn't always so much in what you do as why you do it. You can pound nails through a *Realistic* life gift to make a living, or you can pound nails through the spiritual gift of *helps* to show God's love to a needy family by building them a house. If you actively use your spiritual gifts, you're being God's hands on earth.

YOU GOT THE "RIGHT" GIFTS, RIGHT?

Go back to Christmas morning. Did you ever worry about who would get the best presents? Your parents knew you didn't want the doll that wets and cries—that was for your little sister. Can you really imagine fighting with your siblings for what was in their stockings?

Even in Paul's time, though, people were jealous of the gifts possessed by other people. They envied the leaders, the prophets, the teachers, and especially those who seemed to have supernatural powers or the ability to speak in tongues, "the languages of angels." Paul tried to show how silly this is:

> What if your whole body were made up of hands? No feet, no eyes—how would you see or hear? But God didn't do it that way. Instead, we have eyes and feet and hearts and hands, all right where they're supposed to be.
>
> And your eye can't say, "Hand, I don't need you" or "I'm better than you, liver." No, God designed us so that we need every part of our bodies. We all need to stay part of the body. There's no choice to leave the body. We have to love it.
>
> That's how it is in the church, too. All of you are the body of Christ and all of you are necessary for the work of God.[2]

Don't forget that the real head of the Church is Jesus (Ephesians 1:22). Every other part of the body of Christ is equally important—

[2]Adapted from 1 Corinthians 12:17–27.

needed as much as anyone else. Some people may think they're the brains, but really—how long can they function without what they may see as yucko organs like livers and kidneys that keep the blood supply clean?

God needs leaders. But the Church can only be led in so many directions at one time. And God needs teachers. But we need only spend so much time in the learning mode and then it's time to act!

Think of the Church as a theatre. (Not a bad thing to keep in mind because, believe us, people are watching what we do!) In the theatre, there's only one director, one conveyer of the vision—that's the gift of *leadership*.

But where would the play be without actors to communicate to the audience? Those are the *teachers, prophets, evangelists*.

And what would happen without technical directors? They're the *administrators* or *shepherds* who carry out the vision.

Can you imagine a theatre without set and costume designers? Sound technicians? The hands-on whizzes that create the special effects? In the Church, those are the people with the gifts of *helps, mercy, faith, giving, hospitality*. They're not as visible, but they're equally important.

GIFTS ≠ MATURITY

No parent gives car keys to a newborn. But God dares to give gifts to baby believers. The Holy Spirit gives us power through the spiritual gifts the moment we decide, "Okay, God, I want to be on your team," but we have to grow in smarts and maturity.

Don't get mixed up and think that just because someone has a flashy, up-front gift, he or she has the whole Christian act together. Incredibly gifted Christians do unbelievably stupid things. People who are really about God's work prove it not just by the *gifts* but by the *fruit* of the Spirit. They are constantly growing in the maturity Paul talks about in Galatians 5:22–23: love, joy, peace, patience, kindness, goodness, faithfulness, gentleness, and self-control.

Exactly what gifts you discover you have, then, has nothing to do with how mature you are. Yet it often takes highly mature people to do humble things, which is why Jesus could wash the feet of his disciples. The *gifts* of the Spirit give you the tools to do a job. Growing in the *fruit* of the Spirit allows you to do it in a manner that brings God glory.

SOME ASSEMBLY REQUIRED

Spiritual gifts are like Nintendo. The box comes with the basic pieces, but you have to put them together. And then the more you practice, the better you are at using them. You can pick up tips and new techniques, too, from people who've played the game before. It's the same with spiritual gifts. *Teachers* can always practice their speaking and learn more about the Bible. *Encouragers* can grow their listening ears. *Helpers* can find better pancake recipes and drill flipping skills before the next youth breakfast. Unlike Nintendo, though, your parents won't worry about whether you're using your spiritual gifts too much (unless you start neglecting your homework in favor of *encouraging* your friends).

As you grow and mature as a person and a Christian, you'll show some ability in most of these gifts. After all, Jesus asks all of us to show *mercy*, to grow in *wisdom* and *knowledge*, to *evangelize*, to *give* of our possessions—it begins to sound like we're supposed to have all of the gifts. But some will be more natural for you. You can see signs of your gifts already in things you do easily that are hard or even impossible for your friends.

Maybe you've already taught your little brother some Bible stories.

Or you can easily spot right and wrong.

Or you've got the patience to baby-sit for the overworked mom down the street whose kids *don't* seem to know right from wrong.

Church isn't the only place spiritual gifts show up. Despite what some churches say, your role as a growing young believer is more than to sit in the front pew and not snooze or throw spit wads during the sermon. You can use your spiritual gifts at home, in school, at a job, with your friends, as well as on missions trips. God can put you to work anytime, anyplace. The key? Knowing which gifts you have so you can put them to use when you see what needs to be done.

SENSATIONAL VERSUS SUPERNATURAL

Some Christians complain because their gifts seem less than sensational. Setting up chairs because you have the gift of helps makes you wonder, *This is so dull—how can it be God using me to do important stuff?"* *All* of the gifts are supernatural, enabling you to do things above and beyond what you could on your own through your life gifts. Not all of them are as exotic or attention-grabbing.

Face it. If you had a *healing* gift that allowed you to wipe out bad hair days, you'd gain a lot of attention and a lot of friends—a lot more than if you have a *mercy* gift that helps you make your church youth group a welcoming place for everyone, nerds included. But they're really just as supernatural, evidence of God working through you to do things you can't really do alone.

Yes, sometimes God uses eye-popping gifts to get our attention. Especially to make way for evangelism. One youth pastor high-centered a bus—that means no wheels, just the chassis, touching the ground—with 70 kids on board, two hours from nowhere on a deserted mountain road. (No, it wasn't Kevin.) After the leaders tried everything to get the bus back on the road, the pastor gathered the kids around to pray, "Lord, we're really in a mess, so we could use your help. Amen." BAM! The bus popped out then and there. No one was more surprised than the pastor—but several of the kids accepted Christ on the spot.

You only have to look at the disciples, however, to know that a steady diet of miracles and healings, nice as it sounds, just doesn't get God's true message across. Close followers of Jesus who witnessed all the greatest miracles—like James and John—still didn't get who Jesus was. Peter still temporarily turned his back on God. No, while God has a zillion flavors of spiritual gifts, the plain vanilla ones get most of the work done. Vanilla is a great flavor—and versatile. You can add chocolate, strawberries, nuts, bananas, or root beer, using it in dozens of ways. God saves the exotic flavors for special places and occasions.

SO WHY UNCOVER YOUR GIFTS?

Why figure out your gifts? There are two huge reasons. First, there's a lot of work to be done. God doesn't force anyone to use their spiritual gifts. Result? Too many people look around and say, "Hey, not my job, man!" Whatever your gifts, God set aside tasks within the kingdom that will make a difference and be rewarding for you—that fit your special design.

And that's the second reason to discover your gifts. If you discover the roles God wants you to take on, you can find the spot in God's work where you fit just right.

Don't toss this book away, snarling, "But I'm not going to be a missionary or a minister," because that's exactly our point! Everyone has a role to play, not just those who end up as Grand Pooh-bahs of God's workers. If service sounds boring, you probably haven't tried the right things yet.

Maybe so far you've only tried service projects because you had to. Or because you got roped in by your friends. Their idea of fun is refinishing all the chairs in the Sunday school classrooms. You hated it. Give service another chance. You might rather teach the kids who'll sit in those chairs, or take them outside to play Red Rover, or not do anything with kids at all!

SO WHICH GIFTS DO YOU HAVE?

Remember, God passes out the gifts as soon as you decide to be a part of God's work. The seeds of what you can do for God are already deep inside you. In the years ahead, you'll grow through study and practice in your ability to use those gifts, but you can already begin to discover what they are. Don't worry about which gifts you have. Whatever they are, God chose them just for you. Here's a process for figuring out your gifts:

1. Look through the list of gifts.

- Evangelism
- Helps
- Leadership
- Discernment/Prophecy
- Encouragement/Mercy
- Faith
- Hospitality/Giving
- Teaching/Wisdom/Knowledge
- Healing/Miracles/Tongues

Which gifts sound most like you? Start with those "well, maybe . . ." as you work through the descriptions of each gift below. Don't miss this: *Then read through the rest of them.* You may be surprised.

2. As you read through a description, think about
- Does it sound like things you've done?
- If not, does it sound like things that you might like to do?
- Is it similar to a life gift you already discovered?

3. Decide for yourself whether it might be one of your gifts, scoring as follows:

1=Definitely not one of my gifts.
2=Not sure. Haven't tried this, but it sounds interesting.
3=One of my gifts—I know it.

4. When you're done, transfer your scores here here:
___ Evangelism
___ Helps
___ Leadership
___ Discernment/Prophecy
___ Encouragement/Mercy
___ Faith
___ Hospitality
___ Giving
___ Teaching/Wisdom/Knowledge
___ Healing/Miracles/Tongues
And remember to record your scores on page 207.

THE GIFT OF EVANGELISM

The ability to spread the Good News of Jesus Christ in a way that appeals to those who don't know him—causing people to accept and follow Jesus.

You may not hand out tracts on street corners or carry signs around the school flagpole that say, "Repent." But you *do* wish that other kids could know your God.

Maybe you wear a necklace or pin with a Christian symbol and can easily tell others about it if you're asked. Or it's easy for you to invite friends along to youth events at your church. Or you find yourself thinking about—and then sharing with others—answers to the questions that keep some kids from going near God—like "Why is there suffering?" or "Is there really only one God?"

Or you're really drawn to places where people just don't know Jesus. You can imagine yourself as a missionary—across town or across the world—and hope for chances to share God's Good News.

DO YOU HAVE THE SPIRITUAL GIFT OF EVANGELISM?
☐ I can comfortably talk about my Christian faith with others in a way that makes them comfortable as well.

☐ I wish others could understand why my faith is important to me.
☐ I enjoy many friendships with people who aren't Christians.
☐ I enjoy studying questions that challenge Christianity.
☐ I look for ways to help people understand how their needs can be met through Christianity.

TIPS ON DEVELOPING YOUR GIFT OF EVANGELISM

1. Study and practice talking about God's grace and forgiveness. It may take some work to figure out your own style and story.
2. Take advantage of short-term missions projects. Talk with people who have done a variety of projects to understand which have the most appeal to you, and see Kevin's book *Catch the Wave!* (more info on that at the end of the chapter).

1=Definitely not one of my gifts.
2=Not sure. Haven't tried this, but it sounds interesting.
Score: _____ 3=One of my gifts—I know it.

THE GIFT OF HELPS

The ability to work alongside others, seeing spiritual value in the practical tasks that further God's purposes.

For you, being in the spotlight ranks right up there with a trip to the dentist. And you may not want to attend a bunch of meetings to plan the next homecoming dance.

But—you *notice* when people need help. You do something about it. And like it! You don't have to stop and think about holding a door for someone who has too much to carry. You dive in to fold and stamp a mailing for your mom's business. You put away chairs after a youth group meeting. Or find out the homework assignments for a sick friend. Or bus tables at a pancake breakfast.

Maybe you've even begun to see that when you act on these impulses to help others, you're giving God a chance to act through you.

Doing what needs to be done without others knowing it—even before they see the need—lets you be a part of God's work in a meaningful way.

DO YOU HAVE THE SPIRITUAL GIFT OF HELPS?

☐ I don't need to be a leader—I'd rather take on practical tasks.

☐ I notice little jobs that need to be done and do them.

☐ When I help with routine tasks, I feel a spiritual link to the ministries or people I serve.

☐ Quietly serving others is fulfilling to me.

☐ I like working behind the scenes and dislike being praised in public for my efforts.

TIPS ON DEVELOPING YOUR GIFT OF HELPS

1. First, realize that helps is an important gift. In the Bible, the word "helper" is used once to describe Eve, once for King David, and *16* times to describe *God* as the source of strong, powerful help. God knows how valuable helping is.

2. Look for people you want to help—leaders, teachers, or others who are active in things that interest you. Speak up about how you might help them. Not everyone sees what needs to be done!

1=Definitely not one of my gifts.

2=Not sure. Haven't tried this, but it sounds interesting.

Score: _____ 3=One of my gifts—I know it.

THE GIFT OF LEADERSHIP

*The ability to motivate, coordinate, and direct
others in doing God's work.*

Student congress, scout patrol leader, youth convention delegate, team captain—chances are your friends already recognize they can trust you with responsibility. They may even look to you to get things going or to solve a sticky situation, like convincing your confirmation teacher to forget about five-page sermon summaries each week.

In a group, you don't dread being appointed leader. You have enough confidence in your ideas that you can get others to follow your suggestions. Maybe everyone got behind your strategies to tone down the neighborhood bully. Or they worked with you to get ice cream served more often in the cafeteria. Or to get your church to let the teens adopt a nursing home.

For you, it isn't about being in charge, but knowing that things usually head in a good direction if you're in charge.

Note: There are two more gifts related to Leadership: Administration and Shepherding. Administrators often see the most efficient way to get things done and can organize information, events, or material so that things can happen. Shepherds understand how to guide and care for groups of people as they grow spiritually.

People with these gifts may also be leaders. For now, what's most important is recognizing that God might call you to lead in one of these ways.

DO YOU HAVE THE SPIRITUAL GIFT OF LEADERSHIP?

☐ Disorganization frustrates me; I want to take over.

☐ If I'm in charge, my friends sense we're headed in the right direction.

☐ I'm in control of my own time/priorities *or* my own belongings *or* finances.

☐ I like to organize facts, people, or events.

☐ I can lay out the actions to deal with anticipated problems.

TIPS ON DEVELOPING YOUR GIFT OF LEADERSHIP

1. Work under someone you consider to be an effective leader—a humble servant of God who motivates others to work together toward a common goal. Find friends that will hold you accountable—those who seem to have faith or discernment—who will help you be a good leader who doesn't abuse power.

2. Study what the Bible has to say about servant leaders. Start with Matthew 20:25–28; Ephesians 2:5–11; John 13:1–15; 1 Peter 5:2–4.

Score: _____

1 = Definitely not one of my gifts.
2 = Not sure. Haven't tried this, but it sounds interesting.
3 = One of my gifts—I know it.

THE GIFTS OF DISCERNMENT AND PROPHECY

The ability to recognize what comes from God and what doesn't—or to proclaim God's truths in ways that fit current situations, with insight into how God wants things to change.

You're the one who says, "This isn't right." Maybe you're reading a book, watching a movie, or listening to a speaker and you just know the message isn't what God wants people to hear.

Or you're talking with a friend and feel an urge to tell them something about their lives. You see an image of something you didn't dream up on your own—maybe a sunrise or a flower unfolding and you tell your friend, "God wants to help you make a fresh start!"

Prophets and discerners sense what God wants them to say in a situation. Maybe they grasp how an Old Testament Bible story is relevant to today or what view Jesus might hold on an issue. Usually first, though, they have a strong relationship with God.

DO YOU HAVE THE SPIRITUAL GIFT OF DISCERNMENT OR PROPHECY?

☐ I often get a gut feel whether a situation is good or bad.

☐ I can judge where people are coming from—whether they're real or fake.

☐ I sense whether a book/movie/presentation will bring people closer to God—or push them away.

☐ Sometimes I see or think of images that convey God's truth.

☐ I listen carefully for what God wants me to say to others.

TIPS ON DEVELOPING YOUR GIFT OF DISCERNMENT OR PROPHECY

1. Study the Bible as much as you can so you understand what God has already told us about a world of issues.
2. Keep a journal where you can record insights, impressions, or images you see and how you are led to apply them. Share these with someone who has a mature gift of prophecy or discernment so you can gain their insights.

1=Definitely not one of my gifts.
2=Not sure. Haven't tried this, but it sounds interesting.
Score: _____ 3=One of my gifts—I know it.

THE GIFTS OF ENCOURAGEMENT AND MERCY

The ability to see the suffering of others and offer comfort by showing empathy, listening effectively, or acting kindly—helping them heal emotionally, relationally, or physically.

Your phone rings off the hook because friends know you're a good listener when they've got problems. Your heart is torn by stories of poverty or illness. And you tend to pick up strays—whether injured animals or kids who have trouble fitting in, they sense they're safe with you.

If you have the gift of encouragement or mercy, you know what to say and do when the chips are down for someone else. When a friend's grandmother dies, you understand whether she just wants to take a walk with you or head to the basketball game with everyone to get her mind off things. You may have felt prompted to sponsor a poor child overseas—*and* more likely than not, you followed through on that commitment.

Given that one of Satan's nicknames is the *Dis*courager, there's a lot of work to be done by people with this gift.

DO YOU HAVE THE SPIRITUAL GIFT OF ENCOURAGEMENT OR MERCY?

☐ I get upset when others are hurt or rejected. I want to reach out to them.

☐ I like to show others how much God loves them.

☐ Others say I'm a good listener.

☐ I often see the best in others—things they're slow to recognize in themselves.

☐ I see how I can help others and can gain their confidence easily.

TIPS ON DEVELOPING YOUR GIFT OF ENCOURAGEMENT OR MERCY

1. Take a class in peer counseling or peer mediation.
2. Find a mentor with these gifts. Go with them to pray and minister to those in need of help.
3. Get active in or financially support "mercy ministries" to help those less fortunate than you—feeding the hungry, building homes for the poor, helping in development work.

Score: _____

1 = Definitely not one of my gifts.
2 = Not sure. Haven't tried this, but it sounds interesting.
3 = One of my gifts—I know it.

THE GIFT OF FAITH

*The ability to recognize what God wants accomplished—
a strong belief that God will see it done no matter
how big the barriers.*

You "know" when God wants something done—healing a relationship, empowering people to start a new program, or providing funds for you to join on a missions trip. Even when the odds are stacked against it and people say, "It can't be done," sometimes you can *see* that God is going to pull it off anyway. Long ago your friends stopped trying to talk you out of things you're confident about. Now they just call you a hopeless optimist.

Maybe it was your conviction that the church would let you paint murals all over the old sanctuary walls. Or that your youth group could raise enough money to purchase a van to bring senior citizens to Sunday services. Or your vision of how a service project might get pulled off, right down to your knowing the kind of sandwiches the church would provide for the trip.

Prayer for you is acknowledging that God is active in our lives.

DO YOU HAVE THE SPIRITUAL GIFT OF FAITH?

☐ I know God is faithful, even when life seems impossible.

☐ I firmly believe God is active in our lives.

☐ My friends tell me I'm an "incurable optimist."

☐ If I sense that God is behind a project or idea, I can support it even when others are doubtful.

☐ My personal experiences help me believe in the power of faith.

TIPS ON DEVELOPING YOUR GIFT OF FAITH

1. Pray with other people who have the gift of faith.
2. Record instances where you are sure God is at work. Reread them later to see what actually happened. How often were you right?

1 = Definitely not one of my gifts.

2 = Not sure. Haven't tried this, but it sounds interesting.

Score: _____ 3 = One of my gifts—I know it.

THE GIFT OF GIVING

The ability to give of material possessions freely and happily to assist people and further God's causes.

Instead of having a long wish list of things you want to buy, you're sensitive to how much you already have. Maybe you even feel a bit guilty when you ask your parents for better shoes or the hottest new jeans. But that guilt pushes you to think of ways to do what you can for those who have less.

Perhaps you agreed to give up fast food for a year to help sponsor a World Vision child overseas. Staged a carnival for muscular dystrophy. Willingly gave of your CD collection and new sneakers when another family lost everything in a fire. Packed baskets for a Thanksgiving food drive. Or you seemed to know which adults might provide financial support for a teen missions trip. You had no trouble approaching them successfully.

Or it's important to you to set aside some of your allowance or what you earn for a cause you believe in. Maybe it already isn't enough to rest on what your parents give—you want to help, too. And you feel connected to the person or organization you support. It's one way you really feel a part of what God is doing.

DO YOU HAVE THE SPIRITUAL GIFT OF GIVING?

☐ I handle money well.

☐ No one has to push me to give to others.

☐ It's easy for me to ask others to give to causes I believe in.

☐ I've had ideas that helped my family give more money to others.

☐ Giving to a cause or ministry helps me feel a part of it.

TIPS ON DEVELOPING YOUR GIFT OF GIVING

1. Study what the Bible has to say on money and possessions. Start with Luke 21:1–4; Luke 12:16–34; Matthew 6:19–21, 24; 1 Timothy 6:6–11; 1 Peter 5:2–4.

2. Research the causes that interest you. How might you free up money to give to them? Remember, it isn't *money*, but the *love* of money that is the root of all evil. Some very wealthy people have this gift—they look at each dollar they earn as a dollar available to fund others to carry out God's purposes.

1=Definitely not one of my gifts.
2=Not sure. Haven't tried this, but it sounds interesting.
Score: _____ 3=One of my gifts—I know it.

THE GIFT OF HOSPITALITY

The ability to demonstrate God's love by providing others with a warm welcome, food, shelter, or fellowship.

You know how to make other people feel welcome. Everyone wants to sit at your lunch table because you steer the conversation so everyone's at ease. You adjust the chairs so there's room for late arrivals. You share your dessert.

If there's a new kid at school, you're the first to invite him or her to join your crowd for a movie or to sit together at the next basketball game. You don't want anyone to stay a stranger for long.

And your friends like to gather at your house—not necessarily because you have a pool or the best laser disc collection, but because you know how to make them feel comfortable.

You know that it's pointless to tell someone about God's love if you don't take time to know them, if they don't trust you, or if they feel unwelcome. You work hard to create a safe space that makes others feel important.

DO YOU HAVE THE SPIRITUAL GIFT OF HOSPITALITY?

- ☐ I can make all kinds of people feel welcome.
- ☐ I make an effort to connect with new kids at church or school.
- ☐ I seem to know what activities or food will appeal to others.
- ☐ If I help with arrangements for a party or event, I think less about what I want than what will make others feel welcome.
- ☐ I see relationships as opportunities to pass on God's love.

TIPS ON DEVELOPING YOUR GIFT OF HOSPITALITY

1. Don't worry if your family doesn't have a huge space for entertaining or you can't afford to order pizza from the best delivery

place in town. Some people offer hospitality to huge crowds, others to just a few people at a time. The important thing is whether you and your guests feel comfortable.

2. Create ways to work with your youth group at church or clubs at school so that more kids feel welcome.

1=Definitely not one of my gifts.

2=Not sure. Haven't tried this, but it sounds interesting.

Score: _____ 3=One of my gifts—I know it.

THE GIFT OF TEACHING

The ability to understand and communicate God's truths to others effectively—so that truth changes lives.

You're interested in learning about God, the Bible, and how your faith can help you day to day. Maybe you've memorized key Bible verses that explain your values and morals to others. Or you read books by Christian authors in your spare time—with no one making you.

If you're listening to a teacher, you might automatically think of other examples or ideas that would help make the point clearer. Sometimes when you're reading a Bible story, you start imagining what you'd like to tell others about it and even how you'd present the lessons you learned.

You may already be teaching younger children. Maybe you help your little sister work the puzzles in her Sunday school paper. Or you tell stories while baby-sitting or help with a class at a local preschool or vacation Bible school. You want children to understand how important God is to you so they can develop their own faith.

Note: The gifts of Wisdom and Knowledge have many of the characteristics of Teaching. *Wisdom* is the ability to apply God's truths to difficult problems. *Knowledge* is the ability to understand and use information that might come from natural sources or straight from the Holy Spirit.

Teens often have trouble recognizing these gifts in themselves, sometimes because they don't want to be proud and sometimes because they feel like no one will listen anyway. If you feel like you have a gift of teaching, wisdom, or knowledge, continue to cultivate the wisdom that you'll gain in the school of life's hard knocks. And pay attention to what James says: "Who is wise and understanding among you? Show by your good life that your works are done with gentleness born of wisdom" (James 3:13, NRSV).

DO YOU HAVE THE SPIRITUAL GIFT OF TEACHING?

☐ I enjoy studying the Bible and other resources that help me learn about God.

☐ I like to learn about new ideas, gathering information so I can pass it on to others.

☐ I want to relate God's truth to life in a way that helps people grow and develop—not to skewer them with truth but to help them.

☐ When I study or hear other teachers, I automatically think about how I might teach the information to others.

☐ When I talk about what I've learned, others often want to learn more about God.

TIPS ON DEVELOPING YOUR GIFT OF TEACHING

1. Take advantage of opportunities to study and share the Bible with others. Volunteer as a camp counselor, church school or preschool aide, or simply work with kids you know well—your siblings or friends. How exciting can you make the materials?

2. Even if you have the gift of teaching, study teaching methods either through classes or by observing your favorite teachers, noting why they are so effective.

1 = Definitely not one of my gifts.
2 = Not sure. Haven't tried this, but it sounds interesting.
Score: _____ 3 = One of my gifts—I know it.

THE GIFTS OF TONGUES, HEALING, AND MIRACLES

The ability to function in ways that are unexpected and even miraculous—not for the sake of bringing attention to yourself but in order to demonstrate God's power.

Chances are you haven't walked on water lately. Or brought anyone back from the dead—and no, waking up friends during an incredibly boring chemistry lecture doesn't count. But obviously supernatural gifts still operate today. We don't always listen well to what God has to say, so God still occasionally pulls out all the stops to get our attention. These gifts are like a wake-up call, holy alarm clocks so we don't miss the real message.

Tongues. In the second chapter of the book of Acts, the apostles—after being filled with the Holy Spirit—spoke to the crowds so that everyone heard the speeches in their own languages. Elsewhere, the Bible tells us that if someone speaks in the "tongues of angels" someone else needs to interpret what they are saying. Some studies show that when modern-day people speak in tongues, they aren't just making up nonsense but are using words that fit language patterns—but words that aren't from any earthly language.

If you never speak in tongues, don't worry. God doesn't command us to. Paul said he'd rather speak 5 words of good teaching than 10,000 words in tongues.[3]

What's most important is letting God influence your life through the Holy Spirit however *God* wants.

Healing. It would be easy if we had a God who *always* heals or *never* heals, but we have a God who *sometimes* heals. Why some people are healed is a mystery, but healing is best understood as yet another way God shows love to us. When healing is made more important than other spiritual gifts, God's love gets lost. Those that aren't healed may feel God somehow loves them less. True healers focus attention on God, not themselves. They listen to the sick to

---

[3] 1 Corinthians 14:18–19.

hear their needs and often want to pray for them. They celebrate the healing of relationships, of spirit, and of the mind as well as physical healings. Most of all, they try to listen to God in each situation, seeing their prayers as acts of obedience to God.

Miracles. Miracles are happenings that don't happen in the normal course of life. They bust natural laws, demonstrating God's power over nature, matter, disease, or life itself. Do miracles still happen? Some people spend their lives looking for natural explanations or coincidences to discount all miracles. Yet if you talk to enough people, particularly ones involved in helping people find God—and especially as missionaries or others on the front edge of the expansion of God's kingdom—you'll probably hear too many stories of miracles to dismiss them all as coincidences. If you have faith that miracles happen even today, who knows what you might see. . . .

1 = Definitely not one of my gifts.
2 = Not sure. Haven't tried this, but it sounds interesting.
Score: _____ 3 = One of my gifts—I know it.

WHERE DO YOU GO FROM HERE?

1. *Test your spiritual gifts.* While reading about spiritual gifts hints at how God wants to use you, in the spiritual realm there's no room for armchair theoreticians. Acting on your gifts will let you assess whether you've correctly identified them. If you want God to help you spot your gifts, get out and do *something*. After all, you can't steer a parked car, and you can't know where God wants you to go without giving your life some gas.

2. *Practice, practice, practice.* Just like life gifts, spiritual gifts take practice—ask anyone who's tried to talk about her or his faith. While in one sense spiritual gifts are dropped on us by God, experience often makes the difference between bungling and breaking through with God's love. Experience makes your gifts work in the real world.

3. *Look for formal and informal opportunities to serve.* People with

the same gifts may find wildly different arenas to apply their skills. Formal ministries—through your church or other organizations—can offer you training and access to people with well-developed skills. Informal ministries—reaching out on your own or with a friend or two—let you apply your gifts all day long. One size doesn't fit all.

4. *Look for things to do inside and outside of the church.* If you're a follower of Jesus, you know that your faith applies to more than churchy things on Sunday mornings and Wednesday nights. The only way to extend God's kingdom and demonstrate God's love to the world is to exit the warm confines of the church and enter the world of everyday life. School, work, socializing, and family relationships are all places to give with the gifts God gave you.

5. *Read* Catch the Wave! *and "grab your chance to change the world."* This book by Keven is for anyone who wants to put their spiritual gifts to practical use. God made us for friendship with himself and others—but sin broke that friendship—so now God is working to bring us back to an eternity of friendship. *The Wave* is God's plan to build a tight group of friends—friends who honor God as their master and source of care and sustenance.

You've been given a place in God's plan to reclaim the world. Once you've identified your gifts, *Catch the Wave!* will give you hundreds of ideas of what to do with them.

6. *Don't exercise your gifts alone.* You wouldn't want to take on the 11 members of an enemy football squad all by your lonesome. You can't take on the world's problems all on your own. Get connected to a church—both peers and adult Christians—who can work with you to spot and sport your gifts.

7. *Read more.* If you want to know more about your definite or "maybe" spiritual gifts, check out *LifeKeys* (Bethany House Publishers, 1996). Other great books on spiritual gifts include *19 Gifts of the Spirit* by Leslie B. Flynn (Victor Books, 1994) and *Discover Your God-Given Gifts* by Don and Katie Fortune (Chosen, 1987).

FIND

YOUR

FIT!

FINDING THE PLACES YOU FIT: PERSONALITY TYPE

Y ou can't read minds. And maybe that leaves you wondering what some of your friends really think of you. For example: Lots of them tell you all about their problems. Others could be dying on the inside and never let you in on anything.

Or you're amazed to see how people treat other people. Like how they handle getting asked out. Some can't turn down the wimpiest geek in the school—they don't want to hurt anyone's feelings. Others don't even pretend to make up an excuse—they just say no and don't go.

And it's bewildering to watch friends wander through life so differently. When you plan a party, for instance, Ashley wants to invite half the school. Jen thinks that a group of three or four sounds great. Friends tease Josh for planning food and collecting 'za money in advance, but Nick just has everyone bring a bag of chips or a bottle of soda, chancing everyone going hungry. Carrie tells you a party sounds great, but later you find out she wanted to do something else—but didn't want to raise a fuss. Tyrone, just the opposite, tells you up front what he wants to do—mini-golf gets a yes, bowling a no.

WHATZIT MATTER TO YOU?

Even when you and your friends gather around a shared interest like sports, music, church, or afterschool stuff, you aren't clones. Even if you have a huge assortment of *many* commonalities, look closer. You aren't as much the same as you seem. You have distinct likes and dislikes in how you live. In how you relate to your friends. In how you make decisions.

Those kinds of preferences are what your *personality type* is all about.

Imagine you're about to punt a football. Do you have to ponder which foot to use? No. You naturally prefer one or the other. Or do this scribble test: Sign your name below with your preferred hand, the one you always write with:

———————————————————————

That was easy. Normal. You don't have to stop and consciously engage your brain to form the letters. But try it with your other hand:

———————————————————————

Not quite the same! Clumsy. Hard. Like picking up Jell-O with chopsticks. Of course, if you've ever broken your preferred hand, you know it's possible to improve klutzy, wrong-handed writing. But it takes work.

It's the same with personality. People have different preferences that go way beyond being a lefty or righty, way beyond the physical. Look at your friends. Who manages to tell the whole lunchroom they found a dollar on the bus—and who wouldn't let on even if they'd won the lottery? Who can you count on to plan a great ski trip—and who just lets things happen?

You can easily tell who's left- or right-handed or who uses their left or right eye to look through a microscope. Physical differences are easy. With practice, though, you can start recognizing your inner or psychological preferences, too. You're born with preferences for

- getting energized by the outside world or what's inside your head (what's called "Extraversion" vs. "Introversion")
- paying more attention to details or the big picture ("Sensing" vs. "Intuition")
- making decisions with your head or your heart ("Thinking" vs. "Feeling")
- planning your life or going with the flow ("Judging" vs. "Perceiving")

Understanding your preferences helps you understand why some situations feel natural for you and others make you squirm. Or why you can have such major misunderstandings with some people. Or why you can or can't be black-and-white about some issues—and much more.

SQUARE PEGS FOR SQUARE HOLES

Talents and spiritual gifts tell you *what* you're good at. As you work to find your fit, the theory of psychological type—or personality type—can help you focus your search for *where* you'll use your talents and spiritual gifts:

- If you're good at *teaching*, personality type might help you focus on whether you teach best through writing or face-to-face—or choose between tutoring one or two students at a time or teaching big classes.
- If you're good at *leading*, personality type might help you understand your strengths—what settings work best for how you deal with relationships, goal-setting, vision, or many other areas.
- If you're good at *helping*, personality type might help you decide whether you'd do better committing to a long-term, set role or

choosing tasks as they come along.

Type is *nothing* like Ouija boards, horoscopes, or being born in the Year of the Pig. We're talking about major, *naturally observable differences* in people. About 80 years ago, Swiss psychologist Carl Jung and, independently, Americans Katherine Briggs and Isabel Myers came up with similar frameworks for how people act and interact. Their efforts were popularized through the Myers-Briggs Type Indicator® (MBTI®), the most widely used personality test in the world today. Chances are that your parents, teachers, or youth leaders have taken it.

Businesses use the MBTI® to help create better teams.

Schools use it to better understand learning styles.

Marriage counselors use it to cut through couples' communication problems.

Individuals use it for self-awareness, acceptance, and direction.

Here we're focusing on giving you clues to recognize places you'll fit in—where you'd enjoy volunteering, learning, working, or even playing.

Warning: As you start this section, think about only yourself and what you truly prefer.

Not what you think would help you make friends.

Not what your parents or teachers think you *should* do.

Not what people tell you it takes to get ahead in the world.

No type is better than any other—just different. So concentrate on what fits you best. After all, God certainly didn't give human beings just one personality model. You can prove that to yourself by thinking about Mother Teresa, Michael W. Smith, and C. S. Lewis for a moment. Pretty different people, yet each has been used by God.

With that said, let's find your preferences. We'll look at each of the four areas mentioned above to get a better picture of you.

EXTRAVERSION OR INTROVERSION

ENERGY—FROM OTHERS OR FROM INSIDE YOUR HEAD?

Think about the places you went yesterday.

Extraverts get charged up by being with others. They're drawn to people, events, and activities—the outside world. If they try to do something alone, they may feel immediately lonely and brain dead. *Anywhere* there's action or other people is better than sunning on the beach alone. One Extravert said, "I'd rather talk to the chair than just sit by myself." You don't have to be a party animal to be an Extravert, but if you get your energy from

- being with others *or*
- pursuing a variety of activities

chances are Extraversion describes you.

Introverts get recharged by connecting with their own thoughts, feelings, ideas, and awareness—their inner world. They're more comfortable doing things by themselves. And after high-intensity time with others—like a day at school—they like nothing better than to crawl for their rooms, headphones, and newest books, CDs, or hobby purchase. Introverts aren't hermits, but think about this: Is it as easy for you to run alone as with a friend—or would you just as soon play with the cat or read a book as call up a friend? If you get your energy through

- time you enjoy away from others *or*
- a few in-depth activities

you may be an Introvert.

Extraversion or Introversion isn't about shyness: Shy people can still be Extraverts who like the outer world of people and action. They just may want more of the same people and familiar faces. (The spelling difference—it's "extra*vert," not "extro*vert," the word we use in everyday conversation for a loud, outgoing person—is meant to point this out.) Introverts can still be the life of the party—they just need more space, more time on their own.

As you go through the following either/or scenarios, you might see yourself on both sides of the fence. But try to get a handle on which way you'd choose most often if you were just being yourself. (Remember, it's easier to operate outside of your preferences if you *know* you're out of your element.)

1. You find out a group is going to the beach. Which sounds more like you?

EXTRAVERTS MIGHT	INTROVERTS MIGHT
☐ call up lots of friends to make sure they're going	☐ agree to go if you know one other friend is going
☐ sit with different people throughout the day, enjoying being part of a big group	☐ stick with one or two close friends for most of the day
☐ eat and visit with a big group as you roast hot dogs and marshmallows	☐ roast your hot dog, then pull away from the big group to chat with just a couple people

☐ jump in with a joke or new idea if there's a lull in conversation

☐ join the group for volleyball, water polo, the limbo, water-skiing, or whatever else you can

☐ get lost in thought when there's a lull in conversation

☐ join the group only if you've tried the activity before or if one or two of your close friends join you

2. You're supposed to work with a group on a school project. Which describes your approach to the assignment?

EXTRAVERTS MIGHT

☐ have fun working as a group, scheduling joint trips to the library, etc.

☐ call a friend to talk through ideas

☐ turn the group sessions into a chance to socialize

☐ share ideas readily

☐ leave the group sessions full of energy, ready to go out for burgers

INTROVERTS MIGHT

☐ divvy up the assignment so you can do your part alone

☐ think through ideas alone

☐ keep the group sessions shorter unless working with a close friend

☐ share ideas when asked

☐ be ready for solo time after longer meetings

SUMMING UP

EXTRAVERSION

☐ Doing; lots going on
☐ Find interruptions refreshing
☐ Outgoing
☐ Invite others in
☐ Say what they're thinking
☐ Outer energy
☐ Act
☐ Live it first
☐ Focus outside
☐ Take over

INTROVERSION

☐ Reflecting; one thing going on
☐ Find interruptions distracting
☐ Protective
☐ Wait to be invited
☐ Keep thoughts to themselves
☐ Inner energy
☐ Reflect
☐ Understand it first
☐ Focus inside
☐ Step aside

If you still aren't sure which preference best describes you, think about how you like to do your homework. Would you rather sit at the kitchen table where there are lots of interruptions? Work with study partners? Find yourself wanting to be with friends even though you've been together all day long? If so, you may be an Extravert. Or do you want to retreat to your room for a while after school, maybe turning on music as background to keep out other distractions? Would you rather work through your homework on your own? If so, you may be an Introvert.

If you still can't decide, that's okay—it takes time to work out all four of your preferences.

Circle which describes you best:

E (Extraversion)   I (Introversion)   X (Not sure yet)

SENSING OR INTUITION

TAKING IN INFORMATION—WHAT DO YOU SEE?

People with a preference for *Sensing* pay attention to the information gathered through their five senses. They process facts, sounds, sights, textures, and details. They know *what is*. At school, they like subjects where you know whether you're right or wrong.

Math—where $2+2$ always equals 4. Spelling—where you either memorized how to spell s-e-p-*a*-r-a-t-e or you didn't. Fill-in-the-blank reading assessments—where you either know the information or you don't.

People with a preference for *Intuition* pay attention to their hunches, connections they make, or analogies they can draw. They know *what could be*. Intuitives rely on their sixth sense more than the other five. At school, they'd rather use their imaginations than stick to the facts—and may be accused of daydreaming or wandering away from the subject at hand. They might want to write their own ending to a story, and enjoy tests that require analogies ("Shakespeare is to R. L. Stine as Einstein is to _____"). They may even get annoyed if a teacher makes assignments too specific.

Put yourself into the following scenarios to see whether Sensing or Intuition is your preference.

1. Your teacher assigns a report on Greek mythology. How would you tackle it?

SENSORS MIGHT	INTUITIVES MIGHT
☐ want to know the rules—how many pages, which references to use, typed or hand-written, etc.	☐ want to know the possibilities—can you write a story, design a game so others can learn the names of the gods, put on a play?
☐ ask for a list of suggested topics	☐ brainstorm your own topic, then ask for approval
☐ want to know the requirements for an *A*, *B*, or *C* grade—and do what you have to for the grade you want	☐ write what you want, not worrying about the requirements if you find the topic interesting
☐ regurgitate the facts you know the teacher wants	☐ find new information on related topics you discover
☐ choose a topic where you know you can give the "right" answers, the facts ("Food Mentioned in Greek Mythology")	☐ choose a topic where you can write on themes, analogies, or general concepts ("Echoes of Greek Mythology in Modern Soap Operas")

2. You're with a group of friends at lunch, discussing what you did

over the weekend. How would you describe your days?

SENSORS MIGHT	INTUITIVES MIGHT
☐ start by telling what you did Friday night, then continue in order to Saturday morning, afternoon, evening, etc.	☐ start with whatever comes to mind first, then jump around from day to day
☐ relate facts about where you went and what you did	☐ jump from the facts to ideas you had or what you might like to do next
☐ stick to what happened ("I had pepperoni pizza—next time I might try it with mushrooms")	☐ use what happened to bridge to far-out topics or fantasies ("We ate pizza out under the stars and I thought, 'What a great scene for ending a movie.'")
☐ describe an event in detail—directions for how you got there, what you ate, who you met	☐ describe an event by comparing it to other events, stating generalizations or conclusions about what you saw
☐ fill their weekends with tried and true activities you enjoy	☐ try to find new things to do or experience

SUMMING UP

SENSING	INTUITION
☐ Practical, common sense	☐ Innovative, insightful
☐ Accuracy	☐ Creativity
☐ Use past experience for current work	☐ Use inspiration for current work
☐ Methodical approach	☐ New-fangled approach
☐ By (or buy!) the book	☐ Create the book
☐ Current reality	☐ Future possibilities
☐ Stick with it until you're done	☐ Stick with it until you find a better way
☐ Real world	☐ Ideal world
☐ Applied	☐ Theoretical
☐ Identify pieces	☐ Identify connections

If you still aren't sure whether Sensing or Intuition best describes you, think about how you handle details. Sensors can often put things back exactly where they found them (the cookies were on the second shelf, right-hand side of the cupboard), while Intuitives may have only a vague notion of where they got it (the cookies were in the cupboard). Sensors may remember exactly what their date wore Saturday night; Intuitives may have trouble remembering whether they wore shorts or a suit. Sensors can give detailed directions on how to get to their house or school; Intuitives may refer to landmarks or use phrases like, "Drive for five minutes or so until you see a stop sign."

Circle which describes you best:

   S (Sensing)   N (Intuition)   X (Not sure yet)

THINKING OR FEELING

DECISIONS—HOW DO YOU MAKE UP YOUR MIND?

Everyone makes decisions, but we use different criteria. *Thinkers* use their heads—they rely on logic and impartial standards—and are quick to poke holes in each alternative. Thinkers live to argue—they can take either side of an issue just to test their logic. They want fairness and may choose to be truthful rather than tactful. You might hear them talk about pros and cons, goals and objectives.

Feelers use their hearts—they rely on their values and the needs of others, putting themselves into the shoes of each person involved. They may find it easy to talk about the good side of each alternative and agree with what others want. Feelers often make exceptions to rules if they see a need for compassion. You might hear them talk about values and personal meaning.

Both Thinkers and Feelers use *rational* processes to make their decisions, but school teaches us to focus on logic and standards. To better understand Feeling, consider times when you thought rules should be bent—like when you broke curfew because your friend forgot to put gas in his car. Or when rules should be firm—like when half the class stayed home all weekend to finish an assignment and the other half starts whining for an extension because they went to the beach. Getting inside people's heads to understand their reactions makes sense.

How might you react in the following situations?

1. Summer is coming and Mom or Dad says you have to find something to do—either a part-time job or a volunteer position to keep you busy.

THINKERS MIGHT	FEELERS MIGHT
☐ set goals or objectives for your summer activities	☐ decide what might be meaningful to you for the summer
☐ decide on objective criteria—hours, pay, store discounts	☐ check out what your friends are doing and see if you can join them
☐ choose something that will add to your résumé	☐ choose something that allows you to help people
☐ use logic to analyze your choices	☐ ask for opinions from others about the choices
☐ concentrate on the flaws in each choice	☐ concentrate on the positive points in each choice

2. It's the start of a new school year and time to meet all the new teachers. How do you separate the good teachers from the bad?

THINKERS MIGHT	**FEELERS MIGHT**
☐ look first for what's *wrong* with the teacher (dress, organization, quality of assignments)	☐ look first for what's *right* with the teacher
☐ judge a teacher as smart or stupid based on minimal input ("If that's all she knows about Lincoln's second inaugural address, she doesn't know history. . . .")	☐ develop alternative explanations for why a teacher may be struggling ("She must not have been feeling good. . . .")
☐ be concerned with how competent the teacher is	☐ be concerned with whether the teacher likes you
☐ want information presented in a logical, concise manner	☐ want information presented in a personal way
☐ prefer clear standards and goals for a class	☐ prefer that the teacher treat students as individuals

SUMMING UP

THINKING	**FEELING**
☐ Logical, analytical	☐ Harmonious, personal
☐ Ideas for data and things	☐ Ideas for people
☐ Fair but firm—few exceptions	☐ Empathetic—making exceptions
☐ Business first	☐ Friendship first
☐ Recognition for exceeding requirements	☐ Praise for personal effort
☐ Analyze	☐ Sympathize
☐ Impartial	☐ Subjective
☐ Decide with head	☐ Decide with heart
☐ Find the flaw	☐ Find the positive
☐ Reasons	☐ Values

If you are still undecided, consider what you do when friends tell you about problems they're having. Thinkers often analyze the situation and offer advice, even giving opinions on what their friends did wrong so they'll avoid making the same mistakes. Feelers may offer sympathy and even focus on what their friends did right. Thinkers and Feelers don't even speak the same language—("I don't *think* you should have done that." "Well, I don't *feel* that way at all!").

Circle which describes you best:

    T (Thinking)   F (Feeling)   X (Not sure yet)

JUDGING OR PERCEIVING

PLANNING—WORK BEFORE PLAY OR GO WITH THE FLOW?

Somewhere in middle school, as you were given more responsibility for completing your homework and chores (that is, you were allowed to suffer the consequences), you probably noticed that your friends approached life in one of two ways. *Judgers* (who are *not* judgmental—we've got a different meaning here) plan their work and work their plan. They dig in on assignments so they can head to the mall knowing it's all done. They don't pull all-nighters and they just seem to know how much time a task will take—"How can you sleep if all that work's still hanging over your head?" Judgers hate wasting time or being late. They make decisions quickly and stick to them—trying on sweaters, for example, only until they find one they like enough to buy.

Perceivers (who are *not* more perceptive) take advantage of the moment. If it's a nice day, why would you do homework before shooting hoops? After all, the weather could get worse—"How can you concentrate when the sun is shining?" They may not work on an assignment until they feel inspired. Perceivers may be late more often or change plans more easily. They may postpone decisions until they gather more information—trying on sweaters in lots of stores before buying one.

How might you act in these situations?

1. It's Friday, the weekend's coming, and everyone is grabbing stuff from their lockers and heading out the door. How do you approach the two days ahead?

JUDGERS MIGHT:

☐ consider the time available and schedule exactly when you'll do your homework

☐ feel guilty "playing" before your work is done—maybe even checking off your list of things to do

☐ study the TV or movie schedule and plan your day so you can watch a certain show

☐ make set plans for Saturday with a friend before leaving school on Friday—plans guarantee a good time

PERCEIVERS MIGHT:

☐ do your homework when you feel like it—or last thing Sunday night because you didn't get around to it earlier

☐ forget about your work or find ways to work and play at the same time, ignoring your list of things to do—if you even bothered making one

☐ turn on the TV and flip channels when you feel like it

☐ start calling friends sometime Saturday and go wherever with whoever's available—plans might keep you from a better option

☐ complete your homework from start to finish

☐ skip the hard parts in homework so you keep going, maybe even leaving the toughies until Monday's free period

2. You're about to buy a new "toy"—a CD player, a guitar, or a new video game. How do you go about making a decision?

JUDGERS MIGHT

☐ limit how long you'll spend shopping

☐ decide in advance which models or games you'll try based on price, features, or other set criteria

☐ quickly narrow down the selection from many choices

☐ reach your decision quickly—even before you have all the facts

☐ not second-guess your choice once you've bought it

PERCEIVERS MIGHT

☐ shop as long as needed to check out all the options

☐ try as many models or games as you can, not wanting to tie yourself to criteria in advance

☐ be overwhelmed by too many choices, find it hard to limit your options

☐ get as much input from friends and experts as possible—even postpone your decision

☐ revisit your decision if you find out new information

SUMMING UP

JUDGING

☐ Organized, efficient

☐ Planned events
☐ Stress reduced by planning ahead
☐ Settled and decided
☐ Work before play
☐ Regular, steady effort leads to accomplishment
☐ Systematic
☐ Scheduled
☐ Definite selection
☐ Enjoy finishing

PERCEIVING

☐ Flexible, multiple tasks

☐ Serendipitous events
☐ Stress reduced by having options
☐ Open to late-breaking information
☐ Work and play coexist
☐ Much is accomplished at the last minute
☐ Spontaneous
☐ Spur of the moment
☐ Several possible choices
☐ Enjoy starting

If you still aren't sure whether Judging or Perceiving describes you, think about ordering at a restaurant. Judging types tend to decide quickly among burgers, pizza or salads and then make a fast decision. Perceivers look over the whole menu, check out what people ordered at the table behind them, ask the waiter what everyone's raving about, and may not decide until it's their turn to order.

Circle which describes you best:

J (Judging)   P (Perceiving)   X (Not sure yet)

YOUR PERSONALITY TYPE

Congratulations! You've made it through all of the preferences. Now put the letters you chose to describe you in the blanks below to record your 4-letter personality type. Don't worry about placing an "x" in one of the blanks.

_____   _____   _____   _____

E or I   S or N   T or F   J or P

TYPE FACTS TO TUCK IN YOUR BRAIN

Discovering your type is often a brainbusting experience. The type description pages coming up may peg you so well that you wonder if the researchers bribed your mother to tell them what you're really like. Or you may feel annoyed that you're not what you'd like to be. Things to think about:

IS EVERYONE BORN A CERTAIN TYPE?

Your type was most likely part of how you were hardwired at the baby factory, but type can be influenced. If most of a family is introverted, the lone Extravert may learn to be quiet. If your parents are Thinkers, you may get a lot of practice in logical debate even if you're a Feeler. If that's the case, it may take a while to figure out what God meant you to be.

ARE ALL PEOPLE IN ONE TYPE ALIKE?

No. They have more things in common than with people of other types, but type doesn't explain everything. Kevin and Jane are both INFJs. We're both writers, we play the guitar, love to read, work best on our own, and make most deadlines. But Kevin bikes, Jane runs. Kevin did his master's degree in theology, Jane did hers in business. Kevin hates board games, Jane willingly plays everything from *Candyland* to *Balderdash*. Balance all that with our shared faith in Christ, and we have worldviews similar enough to easily set common goals for writing and working together.

CAN I WORK TO CHANGE MY PREFERENCES?

You can work on sharing your thoughts. Or being organized. Or walking in the other person's shoes. But first, celebrate who you are. No type or preference is better or best, just different. Focus on your strengths, not your weaknesses. If we're all gifted—but in different ways—then the best type to be is your own. When you work on your weaknesses, don't be discouraged by the fact that it's a battle to change. Everyone struggles. We just each struggle in different areas.

MY TYPE DESCRIPTION SAYS I HAVE TROUBLE BEING ON TIME—OR BEING ACCURATE, OR TACTFUL, ETC. CAN I USE MY TYPE AS AN EXCUSE?

Positootly not! You can't use your type to excuse inexcusable behavior. Instead, use type to figure out what coping skills might help you in life. Perceivers might try setting deadlines for each step of a report instead of focusing on the final deadline. Introverts might work harder to share their ideas. We included those "Hints for Getting Along in Life" ideas because type helps people see rough spots to smooth out in how they get along at work, home, school, with friends, etc.

SHOULD I BASE MY CAREER ON TYPE?

Uh-uh. Don't use type as the only factor. Even if you research a career and find out most people in that profession have a different type, pay more attention to the tasks you'd do, the people you'd work with, and the work setting. If the career still appeals to you, go ahead. Sometimes being an oddball gives you a different perspective that is priceless to your co-workers. And knowing in advance that you're different is way better than wondering why you don't fit in.

WHAT'S THE BIBLE SAY ABOUT TYPE?

Lots. Well, sort of. Carl Jung, not Moses, was the first person to write about psychological type. You might wonder whether people change personalities once they become Christians and are therefore "new creations in Christ Jesus."

While no specific biblical reference can be used to prove or disprove type, we can easily point to evidence in the personalities of major Bible heroes. For example, remember the apostle Paul—first introduced in the Bible as Saul.

Saul, action-oriented and outspoken, probably had preferences for Extraversion. He led crusades against Christians, with letters from the high priest in hand granting him license to kill.

With his big-picture approach to destroying the church, we'd guess he had a preference for Intuition. His training in law and deep scholarship as well as credibility with the authorities point to a preference for Thinking. And his decisive manner suggests a Judging lifestyle.

After conversion? Paul transmogrified from the biggest persecutor of Christianity to its biggest promoter. But notice how much he was just like the old Saul: He employed flawless logic in writing letters to churches (Thinking). He was driven to travel and preach (Extraversion). He had a global approach to issues the young Church faced (Intuition). And he showed whopper decisiveness in debate (Judging). You can argue—and some people do—that Paul was an ENTJ or ENTP, depending on how you read the clues. But one thing is certain. While Paul's *values* and *passions* changed, he kept his ENT personality that made it natural for him to lead and persuade others.

SO WHERE DO YOU GO FROM HERE?

1. *The rest of this chapter contains descriptions of each type*—ways people of each type prefer to learn, how they communicate, surroundings they prefer. If you're undecided about your type, look at the pages for possibilities to see what describes you best. If you wrote ESxP above, for example, read the pages for ESTP and ESFP. Highlight the parts you can relate to. See if you can find yourself.

2. *Think about your life.* Type is all about figuring out what comes naturally to you. It's your chance to understand why some things come easily and why others are frustrating. What situations are comfortable? Distressing? Any clues why? One teen finally learned why group projects bothered him so. As an Introvert and a Thinker, his best thoughts came when he was alone. Still another learned why taking over the family store sounded so ghastly. Her dad was a Sensor who enjoyed the routine of his days. She was an Intuitive who craved new experiences.

3. *Think through your relationships.* Review what you checked off as you learned about preferences and look at the page for your individual type. As you learned about Extraversion and Introversion, Sensing and Intuition, Thinking and Feeling, or Judging and Perceiving, did you have any *Aha's!* about how you fit—or don't—with your friends, your parents, or your school? Do you see any places where you obviously clash? One girl discovered she was a Thinker and confirmed that her mom was a Feeler. They put an end to many disagreements when they balanced their needs for fairness and kindness.

4. *Read more about type.* Especially if you aren't yet sure of your type, two great resources are

- *LifeTypes* by Sandra Krebs Hirsh and Jean Kummerow (Warner Books, 1989).
- *Nurture by Nature* by Paul Tieger and Barbara Barron-Tieger (Little, Brown, 1997).

Your local library may have them. Both contain true-life stories of people of each type as children and teens.

5. *Understand what you do best.* Look on the pages for your type. Under the heading "How your preferences fit together," note your *dominant preference.* That's the one easiest for you to use, the first you developed. Pay attention to it—a sure path to frustration is picking a career that *doesn't* let you use your dominant preference. Look back through the section on our quiz that described your dominant preference and list below first, how you use your dominant preference and second, what activities, places, co-workers, etc., might help you keep using it in the future.

6. *Understand how to stay balanced.* Under that same heading on the type page you can find your *auxiliary preference.* This preference also comes pretty naturally. Now, to put a whole lot of type theory (like whole books by Jung) into a couple of key points:

- To be a whole person, you've got to both take in information (through Sensing or Intuition) and make decisions (through Thinking or Feeling). Devoting too much time to one preference makes you lopsided—if you spend too long gathering information, you never really *do* anything. And if you rush decisions, not taking the time to gather enough information, you end up with bad choices.
- You can use only both your dominant and auxiliary if you spend time alone *and* with people. Look back at the chart. One is extraverted and one is introverted. Why the big deal and all the jargon? *Because understanding this is the key to balance and the key to being all you can be.*

Use this information to figure out what you do best on your own and where you need other people. We'll use ourselves as examples again. Look at INFJs—#1 is introverted Intuition. Jane and Kevin think up ideas on our own. #2 is extraverted Feeling—we need to talk through those ideas with other people to understand how we *feel* about them, evaluate them, and choose the best course of action.

7. *Put type to work to explain the atmospheres you'd most enjoy for working and serving.* Use the space below to record what you've learned about yourself. Check out the stories in the first part of this chapter and the page for your type—especially "Where You Learn Best" and "Where You'd Prefer to Work and Serve." What rings true for you? What's important to you for you to be comfortable? Do you need people or quiet? Structure or freedom? Variety or predictability? What are the biggest strengths of people of your type? What careers or positions will let those strengths shine?

8. *Learn from your opposite.* Look at the type page for the type most different from you. For example, we INFJs would look at the ESTP page. Sometimes seeing this very different picture can clue you in to what you need out of work and service.

9. *Highlight the "Hint for Getting Along in Life" that strikes home most.* These tips all came from adults who learned the hard way about their fatal flaws. Think of the last time things didn't work out the way you wanted or you messed up a relationship or fell short of expectations. Be honest. Would following any of these hints have eased the problem?

10. *Enrich other areas of your life with type.* If type opens your eyes to who you really are, the following resources can help you learn more:

■ *Do What You Are* by Paul Tieger and Barbara Barron-Tieger (Little, Brown, 1994). A great book about type and careers.

■ *SoulTypes: Finding the Spiritual Path That Is Right for You* by Sandra Hirsh and Jane Kise (Hyperion, 1998). Describes the soulwork that fits each type as well as factors that can hinder spirituality.

And dozens more. That's why we're introducing you to type. Check out the topic at your local library and you're bound to find more on type in the world of business, on teams, in school, in relationships . . . more stuff than you can read in a lifetime.

11. *Remember to record your personality type* on page 207, "All About Me."

ISTJ

ISTJs...GET ENERGIZED BY THE INSIDE WORLD
...LOOK FOR THE FACTS
...DECIDE WITH THE HEAD
...LIVE BY A PLAN

*A hearty round of applause for ISTJs—they
keep the rest of us organized!*

WHAT YOU'RE KNOWN FOR

- Being practical and sensible—doing what's expected and what's worked before
- Doing what you said you'd do—you mean it when you make a commitment
- Working steadily—setting and sticking to schedules and goals
- Liking order and structure—wanting to know the rules, and you're at ease when people follow them

HOW YOUR PREFERENCES FIT TOGETHER

- Your *dominant* preference is introverted sensing—you recall details and facts about reality, especially when you have time alone to mull
- Your second or *auxiliary* preference is extraverted thinking—you use logic and objectivity to clearly express thoughts and judgments

WHERE YOU LEARN BEST

- When you can apply the information—it's practical and relevant
- When the materials are precise and accurate—you might get skeptical if they're too fluffy or play fast and loose with facts
- When objectives and standards are spelled out so you can judge for yourself when you've mastered the material
- When materials are presented systematically and logically

WHERE YOU'D PREFER TO WORK OR SERVE

- Working on your own, uninterrupted
- Doing hands-on projects where you can see results and know when you're done
- With people who pull their own weight—or else you do it all out of a sense of duty
- On organizing, financial, or record-keeping tasks that are structured and orderly

HOW YOU LEAD PEOPLE

- By setting an example of hard work and follow-through
- Expecting rules to be followed—traditionally, top-down style
- Focusing daily on immediate, practical needs
- Taking a no-nonsense approach, often picked to lead because of reliability
- Using past experience and the facts of a situation to make decisions

HINTS FOR GETTING ALONG IN LIFE

- Make exceptions—understand when and why rules might be bent
- Notice the forest—step back from the details of a decision or situation, look for the big picture or long-range results
- Open up to others—share your special sense of humor *and* express your appreciation
- Be flexible—try new methods or experiences, try to understand other points of view

ISTP

ISTPs... GET ENERGIZED BY THE INSIDE WORLD
...LOOK FOR THE FACTS
...DECIDE WITH THE HEAD
...GO WITH THE FLOW

A hearty round of applause for ISTPs—they get rid of red tape!

WHAT YOU'RE KNOWN FOR

- Being an in-depth expert—pursuing as much skill and information as you can in the things you love
- Working efficiently—getting around the "rules and the fools," assessing which shortcuts will be tolerated
- Having a few close friends—avoiding the "social butterfly" scene
- Enjoying independence—setting your own goals, disliking routine

HOW YOUR PREFERENCES FIT TOGETHER

- Your *dominant* preference is introverted thinking—you observe the world, applying logic and objectivity to find flaws and assess truth
- Your second or *auxiliary* preference is extraverted sensing—your five senses keep you in touch with the details of your environment, and you like life

WHERE YOU LEARN BEST

- At your own rate through hands-on experiments and experiences
- In subjects that focus on facts, logical rules, and systematic problem-solving technique—wrapped together with a practical application
- When you don't have to rely heavily on imagination or dwell too much on theories
- With teachers who help you find shortcuts—or know enough to get out of your way

WHERE YOU'D PREFER TO WORK OR SERVE

- Helping out in different crises—flood and other kinds of disaster relief
- Using your practical life gifts—building, repairing, organizing things, etc.
- Through athletic or outdoor-oriented ministries or organizations
- Through set tasks that don't require a lot of planning or meetings—lawn or building maintenance, cooking, driving, etc.

HOW YOU LEAD PEOPLE

- Providing your own expertise and hardworking example
- Supervising only when others don't follow through, treating everyone as equals
- Basing decisions on logic and your own set of guiding principles
- Focusing on efficiency, practicality, perseverance, and flexibility
- Leading if you can't accomplish a task alone or are convinced your knowledge is essential

HINTS FOR GETTING ALONG IN LIFE

- Listen to your feelings and the feelings of others—you might tend to ignore them in favor of principles and logic
- Aim for effectiveness, not just efficiency—in rushing to find shortcuts or do away with red tape, you may undervalue a process or look lazy
- Follow through—analyze tasks you have a hard time completing and learn to finish the important ones
- Plan ahead—in your focus on the practical, you may ignore what will help you long-term

ESTP

ESTPs... GET ENERGIZED BY THE OUTSIDE WORLD
...LOOK FOR THE FACTS
...DECIDE WITH THE HEAD
...GO WITH THE FLOW

A hearty round of applause for ESTPs—they help the rest of us enjoy life!

WHAT YOU'RE KNOWN FOR

- Adding fun and excitement to life—inviting others to go where the action is
- Being energetic—preferring any activity or adventure to abstract learning or sitting still
- Staying calm in a crisis—easily spotting the practical tasks that can be accomplished
- Telling it like it is—seeing the facts, pointing out the truth, catching the joy of the moment

HOW YOUR PREFERENCES FIT TOGETHER

- Your *dominant* preference is extraverted sensing—your five senses keep you in touch with the details of your environment, and you like life
- Your second or *auxiliary* preference is introverted thinking—you observe the world, applying logic and objectivity to find flaws and assess truth

WHERE YOU LEARN BEST

- When you see the direct payoff for learning about something
- In situations where expectations are clear and realistic
- In subjects that apply to one of your interests, stick to the facts, and have consistent rules
- From teachers who are engaging and can fend off boredom—plenty of variety, hands-on activities, and practical applications

WHERE YOU'D PREFER TO WORK OR SERVE

- Working with people of any age in activity or adventure-oriented ministries or organizations
- Where you can make a contribution and have fun at the same time
- In the moment—when you can show up, finish an assignment, and be done
- Hands-on tasks, disaster relief, one-time efforts where you can see tangible results

HOW YOU LEAD PEOPLE

- By finding the quickest and most direct way to move a task along
- Getting others to buy in to your point of view by negotiating and persuading
- Bringing order out of chaos, handling distractions well
- Focusing on immediate results, on action instead of discussion
- Taking charge in a crisis, doing what needs to be done with superb timing

HINTS FOR GETTING ALONG IN LIFE

- Think before you speak—you can see flaws so clearly, but others may not be ready to hear them
- Look at your own role in a problem—you may blame others before considering your part
- Plan before acting—especially for big decisions, put a lid on your tendency to plunge ahead
- Balance work and play—you may talk about your hobbies so much that people think you don't have job skills

ESTJ

ESTJs... GET ENERGIZED BY THE OUTSIDE WORLD
...LOOK FOR THE FACTS
...DECIDE WITH THE HEAD
...LIVE BY A PLAN

*A hearty round of applause for ESTJs—they take charge
and get things done!*

WHAT YOU'RE KNOWN FOR

- Leading—you can tell others how to accomplish something, know step by step what to do, and dig in yourself to help
- Being decisive—using logic and past experience to critique choices, then making up your mind quickly
- Following through—you stick to your commitments and principles
- Having your act together—you set goals and plan to meet them

HOW YOUR PREFERENCES FIT TOGETHER

- Your *dominant* preference is extraverted thinking—you use logic and objectivity to express thoughts and judgments clearly
- Your second or *auxiliary* preference is introverted sensing—you recall details and facts about reality, especially when you have time alone to mull

WHERE YOU LEARN BEST

- By the book, in line with a schedule so you can plan ahead
- When expectations, objectives, and constraints are clear—you know *exactly* what you have to learn and why it's important
- Through experience—experiments, field trips, group activities
- From teachers who are fair, give clear assignments, and maintain discipline

WHERE YOU'D PREFER TO WORK OR SERVE

- As a leader or administrator
- Direct, tangible projects where you can clearly see the need you're meeting
- With hard-working, goal-oriented people who are efficient and stick to schedules
- Where you can lend your experience and organizational skills to problem areas

HOW YOU LEAD PEOPLE

- Automatically—you take charge quickly and provide structure, direction, and focus
- Using your principles, logic, and past experience to make decisions quickly
- Setting goals, modeling efficiency and responsibility
- Assigning tasks and giving advice—top-down, traditional style
- Seeking measurable results, focusing efforts to make progress

HINTS FOR GETTING ALONG IN LIFE

- Listen to others—you're great at convincing people that your way is right, but you need their perspective more than you may think
- Stop and smell the roses—remind yourself of this: When I'm sixty-four, what will I have missed by being too goal-oriented?
- Don't just think about the task at hand but concentrate on people—they may work even harder if you consider their needs and reward their efforts
- Examine your life—are you succeeding not just at school and work, but in family and personal relationships, your spiritual walk?

ISFJ

ISFJs...GET ENERGIZED BY THE INSIDE WORLD
...LOOK FOR THE FACTS
...DECIDE WITH THE HEART
...LIVE BY A PLAN

A hearty round of applause for ISFJs—they're as good as gold!

WHAT YOU'RE KNOWN FOR

- Being dependable and responsible—keeping things in order and honoring commitments
- Helping others—with sensible, daily, behind-the-scenes tasks
- Avoiding the spotlight—joining traditional activities or clubs instead, making a few close friends for life
- Studying and working—putting work before play, showing self-discipline

HOW YOUR PREFERENCES FIT TOGETHER

- Your *dominant* preference is introverted sensing—you recall details and facts about reality, especially when you have time alone to mull
- Your second or *auxiliary* preference is extraverted feeling—you can empathize with others and factor their needs into your decisions and opinions

WHERE YOU LEARN BEST

- When subjects have clear right answers that allow you to demonstrate how hard you've worked
- From teachers who appreciate your efforts and with whom you feel a personal connection
- Through organized lectures about concrete subjects, with explicit outlines and set learning objectives
- In situations where following the rules allows you to achieve results you can be proud of

WHERE YOU'D PREFER TO WORK OR SERVE

- Out of the limelight, calmly and efficiently
- With conscientious people who are as responsible and caring as you are
- Through practical, defined roles—hospital volunteer, club treasurer, etc.
- In ways that you can use your life gifts to help people directly (listening, attending to detail, writing, organizing, teaching, etc.)

HOW YOU LEAD PEOPLE

- Taking charge reluctantly, usually only if someone asks you to
- Encouraging others to do their best, promoting cooperation and kindness
- Organizing others conscientiously and quietly to complete tasks efficiently and by the book
- Concentrating your detail orientation to accomplish practical results
- Picking up the slack if others don't, out of a sense of duty

HINTS FOR GETTING ALONG IN LIFE

- Stop doing other people's work—*tell* them to follow through on what they promised
- Pay attention to your own needs—you'll have more to give to others if you do
- Take the credit you deserve—tell others what you've accomplished, especially if they thought they did it without you!
- Set priorities—instead of working through things in the order they came your way, decide what is most important to you and others

ISFP

ISFPs...GET ENERGIZED BY THE INSIDE WORLD
...LOOK FOR THE FACTS
...DECIDE WITH THE HEART
...GO WITH THE FLOW

*A hearty round of applause for ISFPs—they teach
us to be compassionate!*

WHAT YOU'RE KNOWN FOR

- Helping quietly—directly meeting the needs of others
- Being kind—knowing just what to say and do at just the right moment
- Appreciating this life—seeing the hand of God in the beauty of nature or the little things around you
- Creating harmony—helping others cooperate by the way you model compassion and gentleness

HOW YOUR PREFERENCES FIT TOGETHER

- Your *dominant* preference is introverted feeling—you are acutely aware of your own feelings, have deeply held values, and try to understand others
- Your second or *auxiliary* preference is extraverted sensing—your five senses keep you in touch with the details of your environment, and you like life

WHERE YOU LEARN BEST

- When subjects are relevant—not abstract, not even traditionally academic
- In situations where the structure allows for your spontaneity
- Through hands-on activities such as building models, experiments
- When learning about people and how to help them

WHERE YOU'D PREFER TO WORK OR SERVE

- Meeting the needs of individuals directly—nursery, preschool, those with special needs, elder care, etc.
- Practical tasks that clearly help others
- Behind the scenes, with others who cooperate and seek harmony
- On artistic efforts that will appeal to the five senses—what people will see, hear, smell, etc.

HOW YOU LEAD PEOPLE

- Taking charge reluctantly, only when no one else will or your knowledge is crucial to an effort's success
- Being considerate, compassionate, tolerant, and forgiving
- Praising others, not criticizing
- Taking responsibility by following through and keeping track of details
- Remaining flexible, open to the needs of the moment and the people around you

HINTS FOR GETTING ALONG IN LIFE

- Deal with conflict—instead of sweeping it under the rug, use it to clarify your needs and those of others
- Recognize your own value—turn down your self-criticism and see the gifts God gave you
- Establish boundaries—give others opportunities to help themselves. You can't do it all!
- Be assertive—your needs and desires are important, too

ESFP

ESFPs...GET ENERGIZED BY THE OUTSIDE WORLD
...LOOK FOR THE FACTS
...DECIDE WITH THE HEART
...GO WITH THE FLOW

A hearty round of applause for ESFPs—they're fun and friendly!

WHAT YOU'RE KNOWN FOR
- Being friendly—everyone enjoys your company
- Adding enthusiasm—your fun-loving nature adds zest any time, anywhere
- Giving—you willingly share your time and talents with others
- Providing energy and optimism—you look for the positive in life, look past people's flaws

HOW YOUR PREFERENCES FIT TOGETHER
- Your *dominant* preference is extraverted sensing—your five senses keep you in touch with the details of your environment, and you like life
- Your second or *auxiliary* preference is introverted feeling—you are acutely aware of your own feelings, have deeply held values, and try to understand others

WHERE YOU LEARN BEST
- Through group projects where you can build relationships while learning
- When the atmosphere is harmonious, inclusive
- If you know your teachers well and they take a personal interest in you
- With minimal independent reading, quiet study of theoretical matters

WHERE YOU'D PREFER TO WORK OR SERVE

- Doing tangible acts for others—decorating, driving, caring for children
- Planning and helping with celebrations, gatherings, and parties
- Youth, young adult, sports, and action-oriented ministries
- Visiting with the elderly or the sick

HOW YOU LEAD PEOPLE

- Using your enthusiasm to get others excited about a task
- Gaining consensus, seeking input from everyone before making a decision
- Emphasizing teamwork, helping people work together harmoniously
- Being warm and relationship-oriented, winning the cooperation of others
- Adapting to changing circumstances, reacting effectively in a crisis

HINTS FOR GETTING ALONG IN LIFE

- Determine your own needs and values—you may hide your preferences to keep harmony
- Balance the roles you play—do people only see you as "everyone's friend" or do you show your competent side?
- Pinpoint your priorities—in your efforts to help everyone and bring enjoyment to all, you might not take time to plan for the future
- Nurture your spiritual side—your wonderful spontaneity may cause you to neglect God

ESFJ

ESFJs...GET ENERGIZED BY THE OUTSIDE WORLD
...LOOK FOR THE FACTS
...DECIDE WITH THE HEART
...LIVE BY A PLAN

A hearty round of applause for ESFJs—they make the rest of us feel welcome!

WHAT YOU'RE KNOWN FOR

- Working for harmony—wanting everyone to get along and fit in
- Following through—staying organized and keeping your promises
- Helping out—seeing what friends need and doing the right thing
- Accepting structure—unless traditions or rules are heartless

HOW YOUR PREFERENCES FIT TOGETHER

- Your *dominant* preference is extraverted feeling—you can empathize with others and factor their needs into your decisions and opinions
- Your second or *auxiliary* preference is introverted sensing—you recall details and facts about reality, especially when you have time alone to mull

WHERE YOU LEARN BEST

- In structured situations where you can schedule and complete your work
- When you like your teachers and understand their expectations
- From teachers who offer praise, not criticism
- Through group experiences (unless distracted by friendships)

WHERE YOU'D PREFER TO WORK OR SERVE

- Organizing others to get something done, from social events to food shelf drives

- Hospitality responsibilities (welcoming, decorating, social activities, etc.)
- Visiting with senior citizens, shut-ins, the sick, etc.
- With people who are conscientious, sensitive, and appreciative

HOW YOU LEAD PEOPLE
- Taking charge yet taking care of others
- Building relationships before tackling tasks
- Including everyone in each decision, inviting others to help out
- Setting an example of hard work and follow-through
- Keeping things organized, on schedule, and by the rules

HINTS FOR GETTING ALONG IN LIFE
- Listen to others—you may be better at *telling* them what they need than *hearing* their needs
- Recognize your needs—you may be so willing to help others that you wear yourself out
- Keep some things private—occasionally say less than you know
- Balance tasks and people—people are your number-one value, but you also have to get things done

INFJ

INFJs...GET ENERGIZED BY THE INSIDE WORLD
...LOOK FOR THE POSSIBILITIES
...DECIDE WITH THE HEART
...LIVE BY A PLAN

A hearty round of applause for INFJs—they help us see the future!

WHAT YOU'RE KNOWN FOR

- Looking ahead—coming up with new ideas about causes that matter to people
- Following through—modeling integrity and consistency
- Organizing—seeing how people can best complete tasks and enjoy the process
- Being creative—providing insight and imagination, especially about what matters to those around you

HOW YOUR PREFERENCES FIT TOGETHER

- Your *dominant* preference is introverted intuition—you envision insights and interpret facts to create new ideas and solutions
- Your second or *auxiliary* preference is extraverted feeling—you can empathize with others and factor their needs into your decisions and opinions

WHERE YOU LEARN BEST

- When teachers act as mentors or take a personal interest in you
- If reading and writing are involved
- By going beyond the requirements, researching beyond the facts to the possibilities
- In conceptual rather than practical classes

WHERE YOU'D PREFER TO WORK OR SERVE

- Through words, oral or written, to impact ideas and help things change for the better

- Leading small groups or teaching—so others can grow and develop
- Where you can be creative—do something original, think outside the box
- With people who are cooperative, organized, and focused on values

HOW YOU LEAD PEOPLE

- Creating mutual trust among people
- Working for cooperation instead of demanding it
- Inspiring others with your ideas and goals
- Facilitating rather than providing top-down leadership
- Seeing everyone's potential, trying to get them to do their best

HINTS FOR GETTING ALONG IN LIFE

- Let others in—share some of your insights and your thinking process along the way to gain support
- Tell others what you can do—not everyone automatically recognizes your strengths
- Listen to others—while you often *do* know what is best, ask yourself, "What does it mean if they *are* right?"
- Ask for help—you'll face things in life you can't solve on your own, painful as that fact is!

INFP

INFPs... GET ENERGIZED BY THE INSIDE WORLD
...LOOK FOR THE POSSIBILITIES
...DECIDE WITH THE HEART
...GO WITH THE FLOW

*A hearty round of applause for INFPs—they remind us
what the world can be!*

WHAT YOU'RE KNOWN FOR
- Being lost in thought—you focus deeply on your values and feelings
- Being optimistic—you encourage others to work toward a perfect world
- Drawing people together—creating a common purpose, harmony, and acceptance for all
- Having a vision—helping others see the possibilities, persuading them to honor values

HOW YOUR PREFERENCES FIT TOGETHER
- Your *dominant* preference is introverted feeling—you are acutely aware of your own feelings, have deeply held values, and try to understand others
- Your second or *auxiliary* preference is extraverted intuition—the world around you inspires you with ideas for the future, insights about what is possible

WHERE YOU LEARN BEST
- Where creativity is rewarded and you have some leeway in how you complete assignments
- If the teacher takes a personal interest in you
- When you enjoy the subject and value what you are learning
- Through the arts—creative writing, music, art, theatre

WHERE YOU'D PREFER TO WORK OR SERVE

- Where there is calm, quiet, cooperation, and flexibility
- Through your artistic skills—music, dance, art, writing, decorating, crafts, etc.
- One-on-one, through prayer, counseling, or coaching
- Close to home so you can be spontaneous, any time you're inspired to help

HOW YOU LEAD PEOPLE

- Providing a vision, inspiring others to do right
- Holding people and organizations accountable to their mission
- Helping everyone reach their full potential, encouraging them to act on their ideals
- Facilitating rather than dictating, creating a unique approach to leadership
- Offering praise instead of criticism

HINTS FOR GETTING ALONG IN LIFE

- Tell it like it is—sometimes you have messages or criticisms others need to hear
- Watch your idealism—it can sometimes benefit from a dose of reality
- Reconsider the stances you take—perhaps another person's position is better for his or her situation
- Let go of perfection—some jobs are *not* worth doing well

ENFP

ENFPs...GET ENERGIZED BY THE OUTSIDE WORLD
...LOOK FOR THE POSSIBILITIES
...DECIDE WITH THE HEART
...GO WITH THE FLOW

A hearty round of applause for ENFPs—they inspire us!

WHAT YOU'RE KNOWN FOR

- Valuing everyone—you're interested in all kinds of people and activities
- Sharing resources—you know everyone and how to get information on everything
- Adding vision and zest—you energize others to start new projects, champion new causes
- Being warm and appreciative—you can't help making new friends

HOW YOUR PREFERENCES FIT TOGETHER

- Your *dominant* preference is extraverted intuition—the world around you inspires you with ideas for the future, insights about what is possible
- Your second or *auxiliary* preference is introverted feeling—you are acutely aware of your own feelings, have deeply held values, and try to understand others

WHERE YOU LEARN BEST

- When there's variety—you can observe, listen, read, and interact about a subject
- In settings where there is room for imagination, not just facts
- By brainstorming, discussing ideas with peers, pondering theoretical "What if's?"
- Where the emphasis is on broad learning, not deadlines

WHERE YOU'D PREFER TO WORK OR SERVE

- With imaginative, cooperative people who care about others
- Missions or service-related projects where you can build relationships
- Public speaking, evangelism, promoting what you believe in so others join the cause
- Where you have variety, challenge, and freedom to be yourself

HOW YOU LEAD PEOPLE

- Using your charm and charisma to get others started
- Motivating and encouraging everyone to be all they can be
- Doing your best to include everyone
- Providing original, ingenious ideas
- Starting new efforts, then moving on to the next

HINTS FOR GETTING ALONG IN LIFE

- Find your limits—learn to manage your time and take care of yourself, recognizing fatigue and stress signs
- Narrow your options—work with someone who is good at making decisions and master skills for bringing closure
- Face the facts—stay alert to the things you can't change in a situation. Sometimes reality demands respect
- Be wary of new fads—not every new idea or leader is worthy of your enthusiasm. Use your values to weigh their promises

ENFJ

ENFJs...GET ENERGIZED BY THE OUTSIDE WORLD
...LOOK FOR THE POSSIBILITIES
...DECIDE WITH THE HEART
...LIVE BY A PLAN

A hearty round of applause for ENFJs—they see all that you can be!

WHAT YOU'RE KNOWN FOR

- Leading—you naturally start organizing so that things get done
- Encouraging—you support others and help them become all they can be
- Calling for integrity—monitoring values, inviting others to live up to their ideals
- Seeing what could be—how organizations should treat people, believing in the positive nature of people

HOW YOUR PREFERENCES FIT TOGETHER

- Your *dominant* preference is extraverted feeling—you can empathize with others and factor their needs into your decisions and opinions
- Your second or *auxiliary* preference is introverted intuition—you envision insights and interpret facts to create new ideas and solutions

WHERE YOU LEARN BEST

- When subjects are people-oriented, discussing the needs, yearnings, and destiny of humankind
- If hard work results in personal recognition from your teachers
- If you can discuss what you're learning and interact with friends
- From warmhearted teachers who clearly communicate rules and rewards

WHERE YOU'D PREFER TO WORK OR SERVE

- With people-oriented activities or ministries that produce results
- Up front—teaching, leading, persuading, encouraging others
- Creating atmospheres that include people, organizing fellowship activities that help people get along and have fun
- Promoting change so that ministries or activities meet the large-scale needs of people

HOW YOU LEAD PEOPLE

- Participating as you manage people and projects
- Challenging people and organizations to keep their actions in line with their values
- Modeling exemplary behavior
- Inspiring others to seek change
- Being responsive to the needs of individuals even in large-scale efforts

HINTS FOR GETTING ALONG IN LIFE

- Don't take things personally—ask, "How would a sensible, impartial person use this criticism?"
- Get down to business—watch your emphasis on relationship, since some people just want to get the task done
- Monitor your bossiness—you can be persuasive with your *shoulds* and *oughts*, but when overdone your stand may cost you more than it's worth
- Accept less than perfect outcomes—cooperation can fail if others aren't playing by your rules, no matter how hard you try

INTJ

INTJs...GET ENERGIZED BY THE INSIDE WORLD
...LOOK FOR THE POSSIBILITIES
...DECIDE WITH THE HEAD
...LIVE BY A PLAN

A hearty round of applause for INTJs—they help us
envision a better way!

WHAT YOU'RE KNOWN FOR

- Being independent—reaching your own conclusions, being sure of their worth
- Seeing what will be—generating possibilities and your own vision of the future
- Changing the system—organizing, planning, working alone to meet your long-term goals
- Valuing intellect and individualism—setting your own standards for achievement, confident in your belief system

HOW YOUR PREFERENCES FIT TOGETHER

- Your *dominant* preference is introverted intuition—you envision insights and interpret facts to create new ideas and solutions
- Your second or *auxiliary* preference is extraverted thinking—you use logic and objectivity to express thoughts and judgments clearly

WHERE YOU LEARN BEST

- In settings where you're allowed to take your own approach and choose what you'll study
- From teachers who challenge you and ask for extra effort
- Through open-ended assignments, not rote learning
- When subjects are theoretical, systems-oriented

WHERE YOU'D PREFER TO WORK OR SERVE

- With smart, effective people who take a long-term view when solving problems
- As teacher or coach, especially for those who value learning
- Planning efforts, finding new approaches to traditional activities or ministries
- Where you can work independently, creatively, and accomplish your goals

HOW YOU LEAD PEOPLE

- Dreaming up, designing, and building new ways of thinking and doing
- Reorganizing the whole system if necessary
- Being a force for change by the power of your ideas
- Challenging yourself and others to work toward goals
- Making decisions efficiently, seeing patterns and systems that will solve complex problems

HINTS FOR GETTING ALONG IN LIFE

- Share your ideas—bring others into your thinking before you work it all out so you can gain their commitment
- Listen to others—write down their ideas and consider their merit instead of just tossing them out
- Be patient—not everyone can grasp concepts as quickly as you can. Rethink how you might present information so people can catch on
- Let others help—you'll have time to do more of the things you *really* want to do

INTP

INTPs...GET ENERGIZED BY THE INSIDE WORLD
...LOOK FOR THE POSSIBILITIES
...DECIDE WITH THE HEAD
...GO WITH THE FLOW

A hearty round of applause for INTPs—they help us define what is true!

WHAT YOU'RE KNOWN FOR

- Thinking—coming up with logical systems and frameworks to understand issues
- Finding the truth—asking "Why?" and pointing out flaws, applying critical analysis to problems
- Being independent—perhaps preferring your own thoughts to the company of others
- Mastering the complex—enjoying theories, systems, and models, developing your own to explain the truth

HOW YOUR PREFERENCES FIT TOGETHER

- Your *dominant* preference is introverted thinking—you observe the world, applying logic and objectivity to find the flaws and assess the truth
- Your second or *auxiliary* preference is extraverted intuition—the world around you inspires you with ideas for the future, insights about what is possible

WHERE YOU LEARN BEST

- When you're respected for "finding the flaws" in the thinking of others
- From competent teachers who treat you as an equal, allow you to challenge them
- Through independent study, specializing in what interests you
- In scientific-oriented subjects

WHERE YOU'D PREFER TO WORK OR SERVE

- Working to solve complex problems
- Researching, defining, and developing a ministry or outreach—discovering, say, the three keys to attracting other teens to volunteer
- Where you can have independence, flexibility, and privacy
- Reviewing past programs, classes, outreaches, events, etc., to determine what worked and what didn't

HOW YOU LEAD PEOPLE

- Influencing through theoretical ideas and your ability to analyze problems
- Making decisions from a sound, logical foundation
- Winning respect through your expertise, preferring to work with other experts
- Interacting at an intellectual rather than personal level
- Preferring that everyone work independently, systematically, so that efforts add up to the whole

HINTS FOR GETTING ALONG IN LIFE

- Avoid being an intellectual snob—other people excel at emotional, interpersonal, and intrapersonal intelligence
- Think before you speak—not everyone can handle being critiqued or hearing why their logic is flawed
- Warm up and lighten up—you may come across as uncaring. Remember, most work in life involves others
- Take people breaks—purposely join committees or sports teams to get out of your head and into reality

ENTP

ENTPs...GET ENERGIZED BY THE OUTSIDE WORLD
...LOOK FOR THE POSSIBILITIES
...DECIDE WITH THE HEAD
...GO WITH THE FLOW

*A hearty round of applause for ENTPs—they lead
us into the unknown!*

WHAT YOU'RE KNOWN FOR

- Being confident—overcoming challenges where others see only barriers
- Starting things—leading new projects, ideas, efforts with enthusiasm
- Developing strategies—solving problems through insight and imagination
- Taking risks—enjoying life on the edge

HOW YOUR PREFERENCES FIT TOGETHER

- Your *dominant* preference is extraverted intuition—the world around you inspires you with ideas for the future, insights about what is possible
- Your second or *auxiliary* preference is introverted thinking—you observe the world, applying logic and objectivity to find flaws and assess truth

WHERE YOU LEARN BEST

- By studying concepts, not facts
- When subjects are interesting, spurring you on to dig deeper
- From teachers who allow you to challenge their positions, match wits
- If you have an audience—through speeches, debate, or peers who admire your opinions and theories

WHERE YOU'D PREFER TO WORK OR SERVE

- On unusual projects or outreaches
- Where things are changing, helping to develop strategies and solve complex problems
- Flexible, challenging, unbureaucratic efforts
- Up front or at the front—marketing and promoting spiritual efforts, on the mission field, or on global efforts like solving hunger

HOW YOU LEAD PEOPLE

- Challenging and encouraging people to excel
- Persuading others, speaking out for change
- Accepting the risk for new ideas and approaches, planning systems to meet needs
- Encouraging independence in others
- Envisioning what could be and modeling how to get there

HINTS FOR GETTING ALONG IN LIFE

- Cooperate—you thrive on competition but understand how your success depends on the efforts of others
- Be straightforward—state reality without resorting to confusing systems and models
- Follow the rules occasionally—do the right thing instead of taking advantage of loopholes or going around someone
- Know your limits—let go of something before chasing new opportunities. Take time to rest!

ENTJ

ENTJs... GET ENERGIZED BY THE OUTSIDE WORLD
...LOOK FOR THE POSSIBILITIES
...DECIDE WITH THE HEAD
...LIVE BY A PLAN

*A hearty round of applause for ENTJs—they bring
people and plans together!*

WHAT YOU'RE KNOWN FOR

- Leading—through structures and strategies that meet goals
- Planning—thinking long-term, setting goals, and providing the energy to meet them
- Solving problems—analyzing the possibilities and envisioning efficient solutions, whether it's your problem or someone else's
- Understanding—developing intellectual insights about systems and organizations

HOW YOUR PREFERENCES FIT TOGETHER

- Your *dominant* preference is extraverted thinking—you use logic and objectivity to express thoughts and judgments clearly
- Your second or *auxiliary* preference is introverted intuition—you envision insights and interpret facts to create new ideas and solutions

WHERE YOU LEARN BEST

- In subjects you know will help you "get ahead"
- By critiquing and solving problems
- From well-organized, challenging teachers
- Through critical feedback, which you view as opportunities for learning

WHERE YOU'D PREFER TO WORK OR SERVE

- Leading, planning, developing
- Fund-raising and other areas that deal with finances

- With efficient, goal-oriented, tough-minded people who want to be challenged
- Working to change structures to make the world a better place

HOW YOU LEAD PEOPLE

- Managing directly, being tough when necessary
- Taking charge when a strong leader is needed
- Developing a model, then using it to guide actions and long-range vision
- Modeling dedication, confidence, concentration
- Standing firm on principles, against opposition

HINTS FOR GETTING ALONG IN LIFE

- Set aside your goals—practice being in the moment and just enjoy an adventure
- Let someone else lead—develop their potential and let them share in running the world!
- Find a personal critic—run your ideas past someone who will keep you from being overly confident
- Be patient—systems and organizations can't change as fast as you can envision solutions!

FIND

YOUR

FIT!

CHOOSING BETWEEN RIGHT AND RIGHT: VALUES

Assume for a moment that you just took a job at a pet store. And pretend it wasn't because your parents barked, "You-can-pay-for-your-own-gas-or-you-can't-drive-the-car." Working was *your* choice. So why work? And why this job?

Maybe you took the pet shop job because you value *friendship*—and you'll be working with your best friend.

Or because you value *leisure*—and this place shuts up by 7 P.M. weeknights and never opens on Sunday.

Or you value *learning*—you're mulling a career in veterinary medicine and you want the animal expertise. Especially the part where you clean up after the puppies.

Then again, maybe *adventure* and *independence* were key issues for you—you've heard that the owner hires just a few people she can trust and then lets them run the show, paying well for high responsibility and performance.

Add *flexibility, balance, stability* and more to your possible reasons.

Sometimes you're cornered into taking a job because it's the only thing you can find. Often, though, you have the chance to choose, to make a decision based on more than dimes and dollars. In some circumstances it feels like you're adrift on a wide-open ocean. So which way do you sail?

U GOTTA B TRUE 2 U

Finding your fit depends on spotting and sporting what we've already looked at—life gifts, spiritual gifts, and personality type. But there's another part of finding your fit that helps not just in picking jobs but in navigating a gazillion gallons of life: values. Values are your ideals. Your principles. Your inner model of what a sails-hoisted-high, both-oars-in-the-water, steering-by-God's-stars kind of person looks like.

And that's the biggest value of values: If you understand your values, you're on the fast track to making smart life decisions. Decisions either allow you to stick to your values—or steer you away from them. If you choose in ways that keep you on course, you'll feel confident about some whopper issues of life.

Values aren't the *things* on your wish list like a Maserati, a personal Lear jet, or a horsey ranch to call your own. They're the *ideals* that determine who you are:

- Values reveal what matter to you. Would you rather take a class that's *challenging*—and where you know you'll probably mess up—or stick to subjects where you know you'll be *competent*?
- Values define your bottom-line character. What can other people count on you for? You can offer them *integrity, perseverance, stability.*
- Values make work and life meaningful. Would your life be absolutely dull or even hopeless without *friendship* or *creativity* or *achievement?*
- Values guide your decisions. Choosing a college is easier if you know that you value *prestige* over *location*—or vice versa!
- Values compel you to take a stand. Values define lines you won't cross. You roar if you discern a lack of *fairness* or *generosity* or disregard for *tradition.*
- Values help you determine where and how you can live, work, and serve. They tell whether in the scheme of things you need *adventure, personal development, variety, influence.*

You might not be able to consciously identify your values until you stop, sit down, and purposely figure them out. In just a moment you're going to tear some cards out of the back of the book and figure out for yourself what you value most. The biggest test of values, though, comes when you bonk headfirst into a values conflict—when an event, person, or situation rattles you enough to realize your values are telling you to act differently than others.

VALUE CLASH AHEAD— CHECK YOUR POSITION

You might think of a conflict of values as a clash of morals—like being asked as a Christian high schooler to sing a choir piece that mocked faith (happened to Kevin) or being assigned books to read that grossly offend your moral standards (also happened to him). For sure, values are about these deep *good-and-evil* insights—deciding what media you'll munch on, how far you'll go on a date, or how you should help people with some of those pet shop earnings.

Those clashes involve values and choices, but those are actually the easy ones. Like we said earlier in the book: In the great bumper-car rink of life, Scripture clearly marks off many boundaries between good and bad. No need to wrangle over what's in bounds and what's out.

Making up your mind to obey those unchanging commandments of God will get you through half of the values decisions you face. But there's another half. You need an ability to pick between two *good* things. Both halves are important to pleasing God. Both halves are important to living life well.

Let's just say you're zinging through life like a jumbo jet. Without both wings, you're going to dive from the sky. Wing one: the skill to choose between right and wrong. Wing two: the know-how to pick between good, better, and best:

■ Your schedule won't let you go out for both the cross-country ski team and dance in the school musical. Do you schuss—or shuffle step?

- A friend wants you to share an apartment after you graduate. You'd planned on staying snuggled at home for a few more years. The plot thickens when you only get a few hours to sign on the dotted line of a rental agreement—or not.

- You want to spend your summer as a camp counselor—outside, having fun, not making a whole lot of money—and your parents think you should be a security guard for much bigger bucks an hour in some stale warehouse. What to do?

The more you know about your values before these conflicts happen, the easier it is to make the right choice. And the true worth of knowing your values comes as you face even huger decisions of life:

- Maybe you're in the middle of the great education dilemma. "You don't know how lucky you are to have the chance to go to college," says your aunt. But your neighbor claims that college degrees are pointless: "They'll make you pay to take art history. What good is art history going to do you? Now, machinists or computer technicians—they'll never be out of work."

- And once you decide between college and trade school, you have to pick a major or specialty. So where you gonna work? Live? What will you do with the money you earn? Your spare time?

Before you lapse into unconsciousness worrying about the future, check out the power of knowing your values.

YOU GOTTA CHOOSE OR LOSE

Alec had two claims to fame in high school: sculpting and being able to fix anything with a crank, gear, or ball bearing. He barely survived chemistry and trigonometry, so he had no intention of taking premed classes. But ever since his cousin lost a leg in a ski accident, Alec had dreamed of somehow *serving* others, not as a doctor but by gaining *competency* in the area of physical therapy or coaching special needs kids in sports. When his advisor suggested a trade school that ranked first in the field of designing and fitting artificial limbs, Alec jumped. It blended his artistic gifts with his desire to put them to practical use. Because Alec knew what he valued, he was ready to act when he saw an opportunity.

Or take Kim's struggling to choose between two short-term missions opportunities. One involved outdoor construction work, which matched her values for *physical fitness* and *nature*. The other meant working on a musical production, which matched her values for *artistic expression* and *creativity*. Both were good choices, but Kim analyzed how her top 8 values would be affected in each situation. Kim sensed that the first one might allow her to develop deeper *friendships*. That swayed her decision.

In a nutshell, values help you answer the big questions:

What's a meaningful life?

What will I do with my time?

My money?

The gifts and talents God gave me?

And where do I take a stand?

WHADDAYAMEAN "CHOOSE WHAT YOU VALUE"?

Wait a second. At this point you might be saying, "Don't I have to value things like *relationship with God, family*, and *service*? Isn't that Christian? What do you mean, 'Choose your values'?"

Look at the different values cards in the back of the book. You'll see that we aren't looking at bad values—torturing small animals or tossing people off the corporate ladder as you climb your way to the top. Nope, we're asking much tougher questions. This isn't wacky stuff you might get in school—values clarification or situational ethics—where you decide how you can take an obnoxious or evil value and reason a way to make it seem right. This is about understanding the core of what makes you tick—the things you value most highly, the things you can contribute to others. You're about to consider what you want other people to say about you. For example:

- People counted on George Washington's *integrity*.
- Everyone knows Ghandi stood for *peace*.
- Martha Stewart lives for *aesthetics*.
- Tarzan couldn't swing without *nature*.

Get it? Values are the compass you use to steer through life.

UNCHUCKABLE VALUES

Unlike your life gifts, spiritual gifts, and personality type, God doesn't just hand you your values. You do get to choose. God influences those choices, but other than some foundational precepts, the choice is up to you. It's part of the flexibility God built into the planet, the room within the bumper-car rink.

Yes, we're all to put God first in our lives. Sometimes looking at values helps you see if you're really doing that. Where does your *relationship with God* fall on your list of hot top values? Be honest.

Yes, we're all to love our neighbors as ourselves. But we can do that in different ways. Who do you know that shows love through *fairness? Generosity? Service? Loyalty? Peace? Responsibility? Artistic expression?* Love comes in a variety of shapes and forms—and we have a freedom to choose how we love our neighbors.

If your values allow you to honor those don't-muck-them-up commandments, the next step is determining what other ideals you need to lead the life God designed for you. There's one important question: Have you chosen values that let you grapple with the needs of the moment? We'll say it in a different way: Do the values you've picked help you fulfill God's purposes for you?

Jesus awed those around him with his control in every situation. It's because he knew what he valued. His values determined his actions, so he didn't *react* to situations like a pool ball clacked from all sides by half a dozen other balls. Jesus was the master cue ball who *acted* out the will of his Father.

Picture Jesus knowing when to talk to the crowds and when to withdraw to pray.

When to challenge the authorities and when to move on to another town.

When to have fun—remember the weddings and feasts?—and when to be seriously somber.

That's the kind of guidance you want from values. If you're steering with the right values for the right reasons, you've got a plane with both wings. You'll end up at your destination: a life pleasing to God.

CHECKED AND DOUBLE-CHECKED CHOICES

If that all seems too complicated, look at what drives people you know.

There's nothing wrong with *achievement*, for example, if you understand what God wants you to do with success. And you don't end up worshiping yourself or money instead of God.

Some of your friends thrive on *competition*—it spurs them to their best efforts. That's fine with God, too, so long as you're still a good loser. And you don't sabotage your competitors.

Others have to be *challenged*—they seek out problems or interests that no one's tackled before. That's great as long as you can still be responsible. And you don't neglect the mundane areas of life.

Plenty of people dream of how they can somehow make a *contribution*—an idea or a book or a cure for some disease that has an impact on others. If the end result doesn't honor God, though, it's the wrong value. (Just think about the books that God no doubt wishes had never been written.)

Of course there are some values we don't want to pursue. Often they're good gone extreme—*leisure* or *happiness* become hedonism.

Balance becomes an excuse for dropping out.

To make sure your values will keep you on course, double-check them against how people define success. Business and media moguls will tell you

"The one who dies with the most toys wins."

"You're a success if, at the age of 40, you're better off financially than your parents were."

"You've made it when someone else washes your cars, your windows, your floors, and your shirts."

There are millions of people out there who have hit these measures of success but aren't happy, fulfilled, or proud of what they've accomplished. Some would even like to start all over. Maybe they thought the Great Race of Life was best raced as a Grand Prix road race. But once the Grand Prix was theirs, they found out that life was a horse race or a foot race—and they were on the wrong track.

When you choose what you value most, you choose the race you're in. As the apostle Paul put it, what you value helps you make sure you're running the right race. "Forgetting what lies behind and straining forward to what lies ahead, I press on toward the goal for the prize of the heavenly call of God in Christ Jesus" (Philippians 3:13b–14). If your values keep you where you can hear that heavenly call, you're making choices that lead to moral excellence—a life that's headed toward the right goals.

READY FOR SOLITAIRE?

Time to do a fun values sort using the cards in the back of *Find Your Fit*. Go ahead and tear out the values cards now. Each lists a separate value. Note that there are also blank cards if you think of a value we didn't include.

The exercise is easier done than said:

1. Find a place where you can lay out all of the cards.
2. Place the big prompt card (*If I were completely responsible for my*

own decisions, this is how I would value _____) at the very top of your work space.

3. Place the medium-size heading cards (*These are very valuable to me, These are valuable to me, These are not very valuable to me*) in a row underneath the prompt card.

4. Filling in the blank on the prompt card with each value, quickly sort the values cards into the appropriate columns, laying them out so that you will be able to view all of the cards in one glance. Do this *rapidly*, following your feelings or instinct rather than trying to analyze each one thoroughly.

5. Place no more than 8 cards in the "These are very valuable to me" column. This could be a difficult task!

6. Next, rank the cards within the "These are very valuable to me" column, placing the value that is of most importance to you at the top of that column.

7. Copy the values in the way you have sorted them onto the Values Summary Page (152). You will now have a record from which to complete the exercises.

8. Record your top 8 values on page 207, "All About Me."

VALUES SUMMARY PAGE

Copy the values from your sorted cards onto this page in the order you gave to them. This will give you a working record to use for the exercises. (You don't have to order the second or third columns, but it can be helpful to record which values you put in each column.)

These are very valuable to me	These are valuable to me	These are not very valuable to me
_____	_____	_____
_____	_____	_____
_____	_____	_____
_____	_____	_____
_____	_____	_____
_____	_____	_____
_____	_____	_____
	_____	_____
	_____	_____
	_____	_____
	_____	_____
	_____	_____
	_____	_____
	_____	_____
	_____	_____
	_____	_____

ACTING OUT YOUR CHOICES

Of course, living by your values isn't quite as simple as just sorting cards and pasting them inside your locker for quick reference. Once you choose them, you have to *own* them, *breathe* them, *act* them out. Not *react* once a situation passes and you realize you blew it.

King David had all of his values down pat—and wrote them out for all of us to see:

- I have set the LORD always before me (Psalm 16:8). *Relationship with God*
- Who may dwell on your holy hill? Those who . . . stand by their oath even to their hurt (Psalm 15:1b, 4b). *Loyalty*
- Happy are those who consider the poor (Psalm 41:1). *Generosity*
- For I have kept the ways of the LORD, and have not wickedly departed from my God (Psalm 18:21). *Integrity, Responsibility*

So where were all of David's ideals when he saw Bathsheba the bathing beauty up on the rooftop—and had her husband killed so he could take her as his wife? He tossed them over the parapet and lived for the moment—a moment he paid for the rest of his life. And while any of us are just as capable of making mistakes, the more time you spend owning your values, the more likely they are to jump in front of your brain and yell, "Halt!" if you're about to make a stupid choice.

So you need to figure out your values before you back yourself into a corner or decisions surprise you. But—if you don't choose the right values, you won't make the right decisions. Your values need to line up with who God meant you to be.

STEERIN' BY GOD'S STARS

One way to begin to evaluate your values is to list your top 8 values in the chart below. Then look up the biblical references for each of them. Record the insights you gain. How does this value impact your life? What does God say about the importance and real-life application of this value?

GOD'S WORD ON VALUES

Value   **What I learned about it**

1. _____   _____

   _____

2. _____   _____

   _____

3. _____   _____

   _____

4. _____   _____

   _____

5. _____   _____

   _____

6. _____   _____

   _____

7. _____   _____

   _____

8. _____   _____

   _____

Figuring out how God feels about your values is just the first step. When you've got your top 8 values, step back and ask yourself some hard questions about what you've chosen:

- Are these wise choices? Would God be pleased?
- Do my values vary wildly from my family's values?
- Are my choices selfish—or self-destructive—or do they sanely allow me to serve God and the people around me for the long haul?

■ Am I in conflict with myself? If I value, for example, both adventure and financial security, do I understand the struggles I face?

PEEKING AROUND THE CORNER OF LIFE

While your life gifts, spiritual gifts, and personality are constant, your values need constant scrutiny. Life changes. Your priorities shift. Your responsibilities don't stay the same. We'll assume that right now you place a fairly high value on *learning*, but once you finish school you may not. Some people find that their zest for *adventure* lessens once they're married with two kids and a mortgage. Pity the family where parents don't learn to put a high value on *responsibility*. And in 40 years you could be the crotchety oldster who values *nature* to the point that you yell at neighbor kids to get off your lawn.

What's the next season of your life? Define it below for yourself—new school, different location, summer job, college or technical school, post-college. What new values might you hold and why? Which do you need to downplay or ditch—like the desire to play away four years at college? Re-sort the cards to see if there are any differences.

THE NEXT CHUNK OF MY LIFE

My current values	My top 8 values for the next season of my life—and jot a note why
1. _____	_____
	_____
2. _____	_____
	_____
3. _____	_____
	_____

4. _____   _____
                   _____

5. _____   _____
                   _____

6. _____   _____
                   _____

7. _____   _____
                   _____

8. _____   _____
                   _____

The shifting values in the varying seasons of your life often boil down to timing. You might choose to demote a value in favor of one that you need to promote for that chunk of time. Go back to the pet shop job. Maybe you've worked at the Slobberin' Puppies Pet Shop for three years and you're trying to convince Mom and Dad that a summer missions trip or college semester abroad is the growth experience you need. They think you need the income. Can you use your values to talk with them about long-term goals? Is there a big future payoff—maybe not financial gain but for personal development or experience—that would sway their decision? How can you meet the needs of their values *and* yours?

Jane did it by giving up being on the swim team—not a huge loss to the world of sports but a compromise to her value of physical fitness—so she could waitress her tail off during the school year. Her earnings funded her summer studying in Malta. During high school, Kevin—by agreeing to stay home and work his next summer vacation—bargained with his parents to let him go on a summer missions trip to Canada.

One final question: What steps might you take now to be sure you can live by the values you'll need in this next season?

OWNIN' UP TO YOUR VALUES

You're in a time of life when you need to own your values more than ever. Getting clear on what you value can prepare you for that next chunk of life—like Cassie and her mother found out:

"You're not going out with a 22-year-old and that's final. He's a man, you're a teenager, and I'd be failing you as a mother if I said yes," Cassie's mother said.

"But, Mom, you know Steve is trustworthy. You had friends on the committee that chose him to work at church," Cassie argued. "Besides, he's only 3 years older than me, just like you and Dad."

"I didn't date your father when I was 19. And that's the end of this discussion."

Just then Cassie's older brother Jeff walked in. "Mom, you probably won't like what I'm going to say, but think about it. Cassie leaves for college in 2 weeks. The campus is filled with 22-year-olds for Cassie to date and your rules won't apply. You have to start trusting her judgment, because in 2 weeks' time you won't have any choice."

Cassie thought she was old enough to choose whom she wanted to date—given her changing circumstances, she'd better be. She needed room to make her own choices, yet she'd be stupid to chuck her mom's values unthinkingly.

So what's the problem? Neither she nor her mother had thought through the responsibilities Cassie would face in college. Cassie still relied on her mother's rules and values. She hadn't been in many situations where she had to grapple with her own decisions. As she and her mom tussled, she realized she valued her *family* and her *purity* just as her mother did and also wanted to keep her *self-respect*. She needed to figure out how she and her mom would meet her need for *independence* and *flexibility*.

You may be looking forward to making all your own decisions. Problem is, it's easy to get so caught up in dreaming about what you'll do "when I make my own rules" that you end up short on time to make those choices well.

Fortunately, no one—least of all God—expects you to arrive at adulthood with the wisdom of the ages. You're going to learn from mistakes, messed-up priorities, and harmful relationships. And when you do, try using your values as a tool to figure out what went wrong. What values did your decision or the situation reflect? Did it cause you to rethink what you value? Have your priorities changed, or did the mistake show you that something else has a much higher value?

And, if you've practiced . . . practiced . . . and practiced some more making decisions with your values in mind—you'll be ready.

WHERE DO YOU GO FROM HERE?

1. *Check out which values you sorely lack.* Think of some tough situations you've faced. Could you avoid a repeat by paying more attention to a value that isn't in your top 8? Some kids lose friends through a lack of loyalty. Some can't get a deserved break from a teacher because they showed a lack of responsibility in the past.

Maybe God wants you to pull a different value to the top.

2. *Compare your values with those of your peers.* Conflicts over values aren't just about sex standards. What roles do values like *competition, adventure, physical fitness, conformity,* and *control* play in your relationships—look through all the values to see what others bring up issues where you haven't gotten along with friends. How could you resolve conflicts based on your values?

3. *Consider the values your parents hold.* If you can, let your parents sort the values cards themselves. See how many of your top *16* you have in common—after all, you are in different stages of life. Where you differ, take time to think about whether you've chosen your values wisely. To get the conversation off to a positive start, you might want to first show them your value list with what you learned from the Bible about them and how these guide your decisions. Don't make this an opportunity to push your agenda, but do some heartfelt learning about your parents.

4. *Compare your values with those of someone you admire.* What values do you think they hold? How do they differ from yours? Any changes you want to make?

5. *Look at your values through the eyes of others.* Would they say that your actions reflect your values? If they sorted the cards for you, how would they rank your values?

6. *Look at your values in terms of work settings.* Where could you work that would click with your values? What characteristics would your job need to have? Creativity, for example, is honored in advertising—not in accounting. If you like nature, concentrate on jobs that don't require living in Manhattan. Brainstorm with your friends on what your values mean for both volunteering and work.

7. *Consider writing a "mission statement."* A mission statement can roll your values together in a way that helps you keep them at the front of your mind. More on that in chapter 7.

8. By the way—in case you lose all those nifty tear-out cards—the list of values to sort is on page 208!

FIND

YOUR

FIT!

MAKING YOUR LIFE MATTER: PASSIONS

Y our life is a knife: You can cut out cancer—or lurk in alleys and stab strangers. Your talents are dynamite: You can use them to build roads and blast tunnels to veins of gold—or to terrorize a city. Be good or be bad—it's all up to you.

In *Find Your Fit* you've unearthed what you do well—the deep-down life gifts and spiritual gifts that make you uniquely talented.

You've figured out the atmospheres that let your personality thrive—where being yourself comes in handier than a flashlight in a dark cave.

And you've gotten a clear view of your values—that map that keeps you on track to treasure.

Big question: What are you going to do with all that you are?

DON'T GO OVER TO THE DARK SIDE

If you want to figure out the best way to put those all-about-you factoids to use, it would be prudent to check with the God who gave you those gifts.

God is so unfailingly good that the Bible calls him the "Father of Lights" who "does not change like shifting shadows" (James 1:17). While you don't get a pair of superhero long undies to wear while dashing from good deed to good deed, God's goal for your existence is for you to contribute something worthwhile to this world. Remember? "For we are God's workmanship, created in Christ Jesus to do good works" (Ephesians 2:10).

That's what God intends for you.

Your gifts, though, can tempt you to the dark side.

You're probably not consciously planning to do anything dumb or diabolical with your life. But here's the real danger: There's an overwhelming chance that you'll scramble around in selfishness. If you don't deliberately make a better choice, you'll try to claw your way to the ice-cream counter of life and try to eat the whole bucket of spumoni before anyone else gets a lick.

If you know what you like and what you're good at, God wants you to set goals and chase them hard—with one caution. You'll only be truly happy if you find a way to look beyond yourself and live for what's really important. You're out of bounds if you maneuver through your world and manipulate your surroundings solely to serve your personal happiness. Chase pots of gold and one day you're sure to drop as you shop. Pursue self-indulgence and you'll watch TV until your brain curdles or party until your liver rots. And if you dangle over the edge in search of the extreme, sooner or later the bungee breaks.

Besides that, the verdict's in. Guys with clipboards and white lab coats doing real-life research have found that the happiest teenagers in America are *not* the ones who wander the malls and watch TV whenever they want.[1] Happy teens are ones who find something they enjoy doing so much that they're willing to work at it. They have a purpose in life. They've found something they're so enthusiastic about that they lose track of time and wear themselves out without realizing how long they've been at it.

---

[1] See chapter 5, The Risks and Opportunities of Leisure, in *Finding Flow* by Mihaly Csikszentmihalyi. New York: BasicBooks, 1997.

SQUEEZING EVERY LAST DROP OF *REAL* FUN OUT OF LIFE

Jesus taught a surprising principle: If you try to pump life full of things that serve yourself, life deflates. Give yourself away to others and to God, and your life bursts with good things. If you

always "look out for number one"

unquestioningly "do what feels good"

endlessly "follow your bliss"

—you'll wind up dissatisfied. Do life how God intends, though, and you'll turn your world into a better place. You'll demonstrate God's greatness to the world. And, along the way, you'll find what makes you truly happy.

The prime question you want to answer each morning isn't "How do I want to arrange my life to make myself comfortable?" but "How do I offer my best back to God and creation?"

How? God's answer is *passion*. If through *Find Your Fit* you're discovering your life gifts, spiritual gifts, personality, and values, then your next step is discerning your *passion*.

Passion is "a powerful emotion. Fervor, ardor, enthusiasm, zeal"

Cool word-origin trivia: *Enthusiasm* comes from the Greek phrase *en theos*, "with God." So a worthwhile passion is anything you pursue "with God." And flip that around: Anything you pursue with God is truly worthwhile.

Passion isn't sitting in church acting holy. It's not the spiritual equivalent of your mother telling you to take out the garbage. It's caring about something bigger than yourself, important to you and important in the grand scheme of things. It's helping people. Losing yourself in God's higher purposes. Choosing not just to make a living but to make a difference in your world. Passion is as life-changing as getting sucked up in a tornado and deposited in the land of Oz. Toto, you won't be in Kansas anymore. You'll be living connected to God.

The enthusiasm of acting with God is a breed of fun that's different from what you might expect. It's better than a mall rat's buy-till-you're-high shopping spree. Or a TV addict's networked-direct-to-the-neurons satellite feed.

When you shift into a give-away-your-life gear, you may be in for some bumps. You decide they're worth it, though, because what you're doing is *worth it*. You get blisters from hauling away storm debris, but you don't feel them so much when you hear the thank-yous of people you help. You lose a week's paycheck if you pitch in with a camp for handicapped kids, but the rewards are better than money.

When you're a passionate person, you may have less of your own time to do your own thing. But the more you act with God, the less desire you have for less meaningful pursuits. Being passionate will drag you off the couch. It may squeeze out other parts of life. But you won't mind once you realize this is *real* fun.

YOUR PASSION RATING

Go to an arcade and you might spot an antiquey-looking machine where you grab a handle and chunk in a quarter for the machine to tell you if you're a passionate lover. God's passion test is way different. There's a bunch of things you *don't* have to do to light up a high passion quotient:

- *You don't have to be an adult.* Back in the Bible, Samuel was practically in Pampers when God called him to be a prophet.
- *You don't have to be a minister or a missionary.* Bet you've had a teacher or a family friend or a boss who taught you more about working for God than you learned in Sunday school. God works through "ordinary" jobs, putting passionate people on police forces and college campuses and in government. He wants them in hospitals and on TV. Or in hospital shows on TV. And fixing

the TVs in hospitals. Get the idea?

- *You don't have to change the whole world.* The cause you care about may not be as gargantuan as Mother Teresa's worldwide crusade on behalf of the poor. God puts big passions in some people, little ones in others—but each is important. God wants you to find your place in the kingdom. You may be pegged to change just one or two lives, or to work alongside someone else who *is* going to change the world.

- *You don't have to act through church.* Church is an obvious and easy place to start. But maybe your school wants tutors for kids in a nearby homeless shelter. Or a nursing home wants musicians for a Sunday service. Or sports is your passion—and you already coach younger kids. Check back to chapter 2 if you've forgotten what it means to work through "formal" and "informal" ministry channels.

- *You don't necessarily have to serve strangers.* Maybe your grandmother or neighbor or little sister needs your help more than anyone else within your reasonable reach.

- *You don't have to be a religious expert to get started.* The more you know about God and the Bible, the better you can serve—but then again, the more you serve, the more you know about God and the Bible.

- *You don't have to save passions for your spare time.* In school, you can be passionate about helping the outcasts make a friend. Or treating teachers decently. Or on the job, you can give the gift of a smile and a listening ear to each customer. In fact, passion works two ways. Passion *makes the best of where you're at.* You find a way to find bigger purposes in what you *have* to do—what your parents make you do, what your boss says, or those do-it-or-flunk assignments at school. Passion also *makes where you're at the best.* You have lots of choices about lots of things. You can choose situations—classes, hobbies, jobs, careers, volunteer activities— that let you put your passions to work.

PASSIONATE TEENS

If that's what you *don't* have to do, what does it look like to be a passionate person of God? Look at some teens who did it in real life:

- Kelly was captain of her high school volleyball team. She used her spiritual gift of leadership—and her parents' basement—to hold alcohol-free parties. Several kids learned that they didn't have to get smashed to have a smashing good time.

- Jess needed a high-paying job to pile up money for college. At first, teaching private tennis lessons at the country club felt like doing time with poor little rich kids. But as he built relationships and listened to their problems, he realized that he could use his spiritual gift of teaching to help them learn self-discipline and goal-setting. (And the parents cheered for him until he was made the club's athletic director a few years later.)

- Talia hated flipping burgers. But the money she made allowed her to study overseas, which in turn created opportunities to do evangelism in another culture.

- Chris convinced his dad they needed a new snow blower. In exchange for committing to keep the family driveway clear, his dad let him plow neighbors' driveways for a nice fee. But with his gift of mercy he also plowed and shoveled—without asking—for anyone in need. Like the elderly couple down the block. Or the mother of three preschoolers whose husband was always out of town during blizzards.

- Tanya didn't want to give up all her school activities but knew that her mom, a single parent, needed her help. They had an honest discussion and calculated that if Tanya could whittle down what they spent on restaurant and convenience foods—by using her spiritual gift of helps to cook more dinners and pack her sister's lunches—her mom could afford a sitter for the younger girl on days Tanya needed to stay at school.

Kelly, Jess, Talia, Chris, and Tanya aren't any different from you or your friends. But they've done a few key things:

1. *They know God.* They've spent enough time learning about Jesus that they believe in his cause. They're learning to live upward (for God) and outward (for others). Sure, Chris wanted to use the family snow blower to pay for a new stereo. But that wasn't enough for him.

2. *They spot where God is working.* Where other team captains might just see athletes, Kelly saw a group she could encourage not just on the court but in life. They don't limit serving God to what they can do within church walls.

3. *They understand their fit.* They've identified their life gifts and spiritual gifts well enough to know what unique thing God wants them to do in a situation.

Kelly, Jess, Talia, Chris, and Tanya are willing to be *en theos*—to act with God—because they've learned it's the most rewarding path they could follow. The effort's bigger than watching *90210* or *X-Files* reruns, but so's the return.

PATHWAYS TO YOUR PASSIONS

Once you decide you want to do things with God—and it's a *choice*, since God won't force you to sign up—you have four life plans to choose from. Right now you can head toward any one of them, but eventually your other choices will dictate how you can serve God. Here's where you'll need to think hard about where your life is headed job-wise, because your job determines a lot about how and how much you can live your passion. Let's explain the options so you can see what we mean:

- *Make it official.* You can be pretty sure you're acting with God if you're a minister, a Christian education director, a missionary, etc. Serving God in a full-time Christian career is a great outlet for passion. But being a "professional Christian" isn't for every-one.

- *Match your career and passion.* Many doctors choose medicine out of a God-given desire to heal. Teachers can be motivated by their faith to inspire and encourage students. Some Christian of-fice workers mull each moment of every day how they can show Jesus' love to others through their work. The attitude you take toward your work changes it from "just a job" to a place of ser-vice.

- *Keep work at work, passions for the rest of the week.* There are busi-nessmen who head Boy Scouts. Contractors who do weekend work with Habitat for Humanity. Lay leaders at churches. People who use vacation for short-term missions. You may find that your job doesn't feel like it matters in a big way. Then you can use the rest of your life to express your passions.

- *Use work to fund a passion.* One woman can't help making money—and she supports a whole overseas ministry with it. "It doesn't make sense for me to give my time directly right now," she says, "since my money lets me finance 20 social workers and agricultural advisors overseas." Or take four doctors who part-nered long ago. Their practice supports all of their families, but three of them operate their U.S. clinic to finance the one who works at a clinic in Africa.

All of these are valid avenues for using your passions.

Once you choose a career, though, you've chosen your avenue for passions as well—at least until you swap jobs or find a different career. Big hint: For a few years more, at least, you can dream about passions and career at the same time. As you check out careers, you can ultimately choose a job that makes you feel like you're doing something significant—not just one that makes you bucks. Millions of adults will tell you, "If I had to do it all over, I'd have chosen a different career—one that gave me more freedom for the activities that really matter to me. I thought I was being practical, but what I do makes it difficult to find time for God." If you find a way to blend your work and your passions, you'll be one of the lucky ones who loves work as much as play.

FINDING YOUR PASSIONS

So how do you discover that magic mix of what you *have* to do—school and/or work—with what you *want* to do—your passion? Or how do you find an after-hours activity that brings you closer to God? You're probably going to fit into one of four approaches. Which sounds most like you?

THE "DREAMERS"

Dreamers are a cross between George Lucas, Susan B. Anthony, and the apostle Paul. They're interested in everything from curing the common cold to helping the homeless to installing new irrigation systems in the Gobi desert. They don't have a problem finding passions. They have to narrow them down to what they can do in one lifetime.

THE "DO ONE THING WELL AND DO IT EVERYWHERE" PEOPLE

Whatever these folks like to do, they'll do again and again. If they like to grill burgers, they'll grill them at church, at company picnics, at the beach, in a house, with a mouse. If they like to pound nails, they'll build sets for the school play, fix siding for Grandpa, rehab homes for the disadvantaged. They use the same talent or spiritual gift in lots of places.

THE "WHATCHA UP TO?" PEOPLE

Another set of people likes options. They check out what different dreamers are doing and pick a vision they can get passionate about. If they like a friend's idea to fill Easter baskets for kids whose homes were destroyed by a tornado, they'll knock on doors for donations. If they think a homeless shelter or food shelf or free medical clinic serves a great purpose, they'll look for opportunities to join in. Pretty soon they'll be as passionate about the cause as if they dreamed it up themselves.

THE "DROP IT IN MY LAP" FOLKS

One definition of sainthood is being the hands of Jesus right where you are. "Drop It in My Lap" people see instant passion opportunities all around. They rake the yard of the elderly woman next door. They train as a peer counselor because they once got so much help from one. Or they make friends with the new kid at school. They find things to do right under their nose.

In a second we'll look at some pointers about finding passions for each type of person. First a few tips for all 4 types.

SWATTING BACK THE PASSION KILLERS

Big, small, near, far, practical, crazy—God hands out all kinds of passions. But you might make three huge mistakes as you try to figure out what God designed you to do.

You can't wait around until you're absolutely certain you know what God wants you to do. For one, passions are an expression of *you*. God designed you to dream about what might make the world a better place. To be bold. You don't need a thunderbolt from heaven to go ahead and act. For two, it's hard for God to steer you if you're sitting still. If you don't do anything, you'll never know if you have gas in the passion tank and your motor is running. Instead of being stuck, assume that if you're somehow using your life gifts or spiritual gifts—and what you do seems to make God real to others—then you're acting on a passion. You can't be far from what God has in mind for you.

You can't excuse yourself from stepping out just because you aren't the next Billy Graham. God needs Joan of Arcs and Abraham Lincolns. But for every person who helps multitudes, God needs thousands more who can hold hands and hear and help problems one-on-one. And God doesn't seem to clone the big-time players—God designed Lincoln and Rosa Parks and Billy Graham for their own places, times, and purposes—and you're designed for yours.

You can't plan all passions. Jesus once talked about a man attacked on his way to the city of Jericho. As the man lay beaten and bleeding on the road, two holy men walked by. Each looked at the man and said, "Ain't my job." The third man who came along found all sorts of ways to help—even though he was a foreigner, an enemy of the beaten-up guy. That "Good Samaritan" didn't worry if wiping up blood and hauling a man to safety was one of his gifts. If you're "on the road to Jericho" and run across an emergency of any kind, *do what it takes even if it isn't your gift or passion.* Chuck everything you learned about yourself in *Find Your Fit* to meet that big-time need.

NOW AND LATER PASSIONS

Superheroes aren't content with doing one good deed before hanging up their tights. Like them, you have a lifelong call to do good stuff. You might want to think about passions *now*—this month or year or while you're still in school—and passions *later*—what you'll do with "your future."

Maybe all you have time for now is picking up your clothes to help keep your mom sane. You're on the track team, you've got a job, and grades are important to you. Sometimes you do need down time—especially if you have something intense you need a break *from.* You can still make the most of "Drop It in My Lap" opportunities. But also remember that life is full of seasons. Are you in a season where you need time for your own growth? Sometimes you're reaching out to others. Other times you're getting ready for the next season.

You won't be ready for the next season if you don't think about what it might be. The "later" passions that will make or break how fulfilling your life is.

Jane always wanted to write and thought she could serve God that way, but it's a long way from wanting to write to a book contract. So Jane majored in English (and business), got a financial job where she could write speeches, letters, position papers, and reports, journaled every chance she got, read everything she could. Her season to write a book came at age 34. This is number 8.

Kevin got around to writing much sooner—and a bit more by accident. But taking English and journalism in college, doing a graduate degree in theology, studying overseas, and pastoring a mob of youth in a church were all things he did to be well-rounded for whatever future good work God chose for him. He's a dreamer who does everything he can to stay equipped for God's next big thing.

So if you're drawn to a passion that is too big for you to handle right now, think about what you might do to get ready for it.

If you want to be a missionary, start by learning a language.

If you want to serve God by being an at-home parent, get used to a one-income lifestyle.

If you want to serve God by changing the system, study politics. Intern with a social worker. Or at a law office. Or with an environmental agency.

If you want to serve God as a doctor—lawyer, teacher, pilot, anything—consider what God might want you to do in that position. How can you be a light to others?

Jesus taught again and again on being ready. "Be dressed for action and have your lamps lit; be like those who are waiting for their master to return from the wedding banquet, so that they may open the door for him as soon as he comes and knocks" (Luke 12:35–6, NRSV). Now's your chance to get ready for a future of enthusiasm with God, to seize the moment, to prepare now to join God at work.

FINDING YOUR PASSIONS

Are you a

- *"Do One Thing Well and Do It Everywhere" Person*—do you look for chances to use a specific life gift or spiritual gift in a variety of arenas?

- *"Whatcha Up To?" Person*—are there certain leaders or ministries who chase visions or missions that appeal to you? Are there roles to fill within those efforts that fit with your gifts?
- *"Drop It in My Lap" Person*—if you broaden your definition of passions, might yours appear right where you are, in the settings you sit in all the time?
- *Dreamer-type Person*—do you find it easy and exciting to simply dream about what you might do for God?

Flip first to the description that fits you best and work through those passion ideas first. Don't try to do this all at once—but complete one exercise right now. Set *Find Your Fit* aside for a day and give your ideas time to simmer on the back burner of your brain. Check what you came up with and then try another.

FOR THE "DO ONE THING WELL AND DO IT EVERYWHERE" PEOPLE

1. Look at your life gifts and spiritual gifts (page 207). Which do you most enjoy using? List other ways you could use them.

2. Check out the following list of skills and talents. If you were going to help with a project, which would you prefer to use? Which are fun for you? Can you think of others? Check the ones that sound most like you, and don't think of this list as complete—write down any these items make you think of.

- [ ] Artistic expression
- [ ] Balloon-tying
- [ ] Baby-sitting
- [ ] Car repairs
- [ ] Carpentry
- [ ] Cleaning
- [ ] Coaching
- [ ] Computers
- [ ] Construction
- [ ] Cooking
- [ ] Counseling
- [ ] Crafts
- [ ] Dance
- [ ] Digging
- [ ] Drama
- [ ] Driving
- [ ] Electronics
- [ ] Feeding the hungry
- [ ] Financial planning/budgets
- [ ] Foreign languages

- [ ] Gardening
- [ ] Graphic arts
- [ ] Graphic design
- [ ] Health clinics
- [ ] Home repairs
- [ ] Interior design
- [ ] Managing people
- [ ] Mathematics
- [ ] Media
- [ ] Mime
- [ ] Music— instrumental
- [ ] Music—vocal
- [ ] Office administration
- [ ] Office tasks
- [ ] Organizing events/parties
- [ ] Painting
- [ ] Photography
- [ ] Political pursuits
- [ ] Publicity

- [ ] Puppets
- [ ] Reading
- [ ] Remedial tutoring
- [ ] Research
- [ ] Selling
- [ ] Sewing
- [ ] Speaking
- [ ] Storytelling
- [ ] Teaching
- [ ] Teaching English as a Second Language
- [ ] Time management
- [ ] Word processing
- [ ] Working outdoors
- [ ] Writing/ journalism
- [ ] _____
- [ ] _____
- [ ] _____
- [ ] _____
- [ ] _____
- [ ] _____

FOR THE "WHATCHA UP TO?" PEOPLE

1. Find out what ministries and missions your church supports. Look at your school. Ask your parents. Which strike you as important? What kind of help do they need? How might you fit into their activities or plans?

2. For more places to get involved in your wider community, check out America's Promise, the organization founded by retired General Colin Powell to help kids and promote volunteering. You can find them at www.americaspromise.org.

3. List where you've volunteered in the past. What did you do? Would you do it again? What gifts and talents did you use?

At school:

In your family:

At your church:

Through civic or student groups like Scouts:

FOR THE "DROP IT IN MY LAP" PEOPLE

1. List all of the roles you play. Are you a student? Neighbor? Someone's child? Someone's sibling? A patient? A customer? An employee? A friend? What problems do you notice right around you? What could you do about them?

2. You might like holding babies. Or maybe you don't want to be near kids until they're old enough to play chess. Some people are fascinated by hospital environments. Others shriek when they see blood. Look through these groups or situations. Who do you wish you could help? Do you have personal experience or lots of contact with friends or relatives that are part of these groups?

Some of these ideas may appeal to you now—and some are adult/career areas.

AGE GROUPS

- ☐ Babies
- ☐ Toddlers and preschoolers
- ☐ Early elementary school
- ☐ Late elementary school
- ☐ All children
- ☐ Peers (your own age or grade)

- ☐ Teens
- ☐ College/ Young adults
- ☐ Singles
- ☐ Young marrieds
- ☐ Parents
- ☐ Senior citizens

PEOPLE WITH PRACTICAL NEEDS

☐ Education (or tutoring)
☐ Finance/budget issues
☐ Healthcare assistance
☐ Housing needs
☐ Legal advice/concerns

☐ Maintenance or repair needs
☐ Parenting concerns
☐ Peer counseling/mediation
☐ Prayer ministries
☐ Workplace issues

PEOPLE WITH COUNSELING NEEDS

☐ Substance abuse
☐ Marital counseling
☐ Grief support
☐ Families not getting along

☐ Support groups
☐ Spiritual direction/
discipleship

MINISTRIES TO SPECIFIC POPULATIONS

☐ Refugees
☐ Ethnic minorities
☐ The poor
☐ Neighbors/community
☐ The disabled
☐ People who are ill
☐ Church visitors
☐ New kids at school

☐ Younger students
☐ Students who need
to improve study skills
☐ Business and professional
men/women
☐ International students
☐ Missionaries
☐ The unemployed

FOR THE "DREAMERS"

1. If you had no fear of failure and limitless time and resources at your disposal, what would you do (besides repeating Michael Jordan's career and traveling around the world . . .)? What is your dream for your future?

2. Name 3 people who have accomplished something that you would like to do or who have had a tremendous positive impact on your life. Because of them, what causes or purposes might you want to focus on?

Name of person: **What they did:**   **What I might do:**

a)

b)

c)

SO WHERE DO YOU GO FROM HERE?

1. *If you just don't seem to be passionate about anything, relax.* For some people, identifying reasons to act can take months. But take a look again at your values. Which ones might cause you to join in with God? What wrongs in the world make you mad enough to take action? Do you value yourself enough to think that God can use you?

2. *Read the paper, watch the news.* What would you change if you could? Which news stories grab at your heartstrings? Think about these things in terms of passions and careers. What could you pursue?

3. *Try out different ways of serving people firsthand.* What's rewarding about it? What's hard? Which do you do best at?

4. *Check out the first chapter of Kevin's book* Catch the Wave! *for how he found his "lifedream"* of being involved in God's big stuff. Chapters 6–11 give loads of examples of how you can live your passions now and later in life.

5. *Think about* why *you do* what *you do.* It's the key to making things you love to do and the things you do with God. When you act with God, you look beyond *what* you're doing to *why* you're doing it and *who* you do it for.

Have you heard about the two stone cutters? When asked what they were doing, one said, "I'm cutting stones." The other said, "I'm building a cathedral."

Or the two insurance agents. One said, "I work so I can make my house payments." The other said, "I work to make sure that if a parent dies, their families aren't left penniless as I was as a child."

6. *Ask your parents, teachers, and other adult friends the big "What if?" question.* What if they could re-choose their career? What would they do differently?

FIND

YOUR

FIT!

HOW NOT TO SPIN
IN YOUR SOCKS

In the early 1980s, Gregor Dimitriov defected from the Soviet Union to the United States. Yet after six months in America, he voluntarily returned to the dictator-run country he had fled, knowing he'd be jailed by the communist government. Gregor received a four-year prison sentence. Asked why he returned, he simply said, "I couldn't decide."

Gregor was overwhelmed by choices. In the Soviet Union he had stood in line at stores that each sold one staple—bread, milk, meat. In American supermarkets, Gregor spun in the aisles. He was overwhelmed by options. When he needed to go somewhere, no one told him whether he should take a bus—or a car, train, or bike. Once he knew he needed a car, no one dictated it should be a Honda—or a Toyota, Nissan, Chrysler, Chevy, or Ford.

Your own choices may have you spinning in your socks.

The odds aren't good that your life will slow down. There's no way to bolt your feet to the floor to stay stable. And you probably don't have a guaranteed bowl of rice and a bed of lice waiting for you in a Soviet *gulag*. You have to make matter-of-fact, day-to-day choices just to survive. Even more than that, to thrive.

And if you haven't noticed, life keeps spinning faster. Remember when summer seemed endless? You were almost *glad* to get back to school. Unless you teach school, those days are fast coming to a halt—your only taste of summer in the world of work may be your daydreams of a swimming pool as you steam to work on a commuter train.

LIFE: FULL SPEED AHEAD

Life's *demands* step up as well. Flash forward 15 or 20 years. You've got some serious planning to do. You've got friends to see, places to visit, cars to wash, festivals to attend, pools to hang around, cliffs to climb—oh yeah, and by now you've been irretrievably sucked into the world of work. You have in-laws. And that nasty annual trip to the doctor. And your grandma's house to paint. Phones ring, emails zap across your screen, everyone expects you to meet their demands first. More bills, more responsibilities, more choices. Putting Grandma's house painting on your calendar doesn't help if you say yes to too many other requests.

So . . . how will you fit it all in?

Some people actually believe that if you handle things right, you'll have time for everything.

You won't.

You have to make choices.

You'll never fit the important things into life unless you make room for them *first*. Even finding your fit in God's world won't do you any good if you can't find time in your schedule to apply what you know.

We aren't going to ram you through a crash course in time management. But we'd like to share 5 key Bible truths about time that might make it easier to put the ideas of *Find Your Fit* to work in your life.

From the start of his formal ministry to his death, Jesus had only three years to change the world. No chance for a media blitz. No sports centers to hold huge crusades in. Yet Jesus managed to plant the seeds of the Church. And develop deep friendships. Go fishing.

Attend feasts and parties. Tell stories. Laugh with children. Have a leisurely meal with people whose company he enjoyed. How did he do it?

TIME TRUTH #1: JESUS PUT HIS RELATIONSHIP WITH GOD FIRST.

Jesus shocked his hearers when he addressed God as "Daddy" (see Mark 14:36, for example). Even if right now you'd as soon be seen with Barney or Baby Bop as with either of your parents—especially at the mall—picture mommies and daddies from the fairy tales of life. Daddies are people we like to be with. They toss us in the air, bounce us on their knees, give us pennies to toss in fountains. Jesus consistently fought for time alone with his Father despite the crowds who pushed to be near him, the masses who sought healing, and his close friends and disciples who had a vital need for training. Jesus still found time for his relationship with God.

If God is truly going to be the center of your life, you have to carve out time to spend on your relationship.

Imagine making a new friend so close that he or she feels like your separated-at-birth twin. You like the same music, take the same classes, play the same instrument, laugh at the same movies, even avoid the same kinds of jeans. You'd never say, "Well, I gotta say it. Life is busy, so I'm not going to try to be with you. Even though we're best friends, I'll be spending my time with other people. No hard feelings—I just think we'll be tight even if we never talk to each other." Sounds dumb, of course, but that's how people treat God. They take the relationship for granted—or figure that someday they'll get around to deep closeness.

God won't push. He's already invited you to spend time with him, so the response belongs to you.

We're not talking—necessarily—about hauling out of bed hours before the school bus drives up. Just as people differ in what they like to do with friends on Saturday nights—good stuff, we mean—people differ in what adds up to meaningful, growing time with God. If the thought of knocking off a chapter of the Bible and an hour of prayer every morning makes you want to yank the covers over your head, you have lots of company—even among the strongest of Christians!

Go back to your personality page. What did we say your *dominant* preference was? Thinking? Feeling? Sensing? Intuition? Jane wrote a whole book on how each preference tackles the task of knowing God, but start by trying a few simple suggestions—which we list at the end of this chapter under exercise 1 of "Where to Go From Here." Chances are you'll find an idea to help you look forward to your time with God as much as time with your best friend—especially since you'll find out they're one and the same!

When you hang close to God you get *constant love*. You're loved for who you are—not whether you have a date for prom, not if you're perfect. You get *direction*. Other religions give you rules *you* have to do if you want to be righteous. Jesus remakes us from the inside out. You're changed by spending time with him. You get *wisdom*. Like knowing when to listen and not listen to your peers and *why*.

In short, you get filled up from the inside out. Jesus called himself the bread of life (John 6:35). Time with God is the only nourishment that allows you to be who you were meant to be *and* have the resources to act for God.

TIME TRUTH #2: JESUS KNEW HIS MISSION.

Jesus knew that his goal on Earth was to plant the seeds of the kingdom of God. That goal helped him focus on what he needed to do—moving from place to place, reaching as many people as he could, equipping disciples and sending them out by themselves to practice spreading the Good News.

Sometimes Jesus' choices were tough. He had to leave towns even when more people clamored to be healed or to seek his wisdom. He had to come down from the mountains and God's presence to be with people clueless about him or his message. And lots of other people wanted to define Jesus' mission for him:

- Israelites who detested the Romans wanted him to set himself up as king.
- Many in the crowds who followed him wanted food and health.
- Judas thought he should erase poverty.
- The scribes and Pharisees wanted him to enforce the laws of Moses—and all the quibbles and bits added to it over the centuries.

It isn't too soon to start thinking about your own mission in life. As you've worked through *Find Your Fit*, maybe you've caught glimpses of what God wants you to be. Your understanding of how God has gifted you and where he's leading you might change, but you've got two huge questions to settle.

At some point you have to make a conscious choice: *Do you accept God's view of the world?* Do you believe that Jesus came both to save us from our sins and to teach us how to live? Christ's death paid for our sin. It makes us acceptable to God. It opens the way for us to have a relationship with God. And God makes us part of his plan to bring the kingdom of Heaven to reality. The Bible puts it like this:

- I [Jesus] tell you the truth, whoever hears my word and believes him who sent me has eternal life and will not be condemned; he has crossed over from death to life (John 5:24).
- For he [God] has rescued us from the dominion of darkness and brought us into the kingdom of the Son he loves, in whom we have redemption, the forgiveness of sins (Colossians 1:13–14).

When you accept God's view of the world, you trust that God's plans are good. You open your heart to what he wants. No matter how dangerous it may seem to trust God with your life, it's infinitely more dangerous to live your life outside of God's will. It's your choice, though, because God doesn't use puppets. You can include or exclude God as you design your mission for life.

There's a second big question to settle: *Do you accept God's view of you?* God is working in you. God has a plan, and you're part of it. Christians *can* make a difference if they understand what God wants them to do.

You can decide that life has no meaning. To rewrite the rules to suit yourself. That the world owes you. That you can't change—that whatever happens is the fault of a horrid childhood, traumatic events, or breaks you didn't get. Or that the earth's already in ruins and humans are doomed.

The Christian view, though, says that *you can be different* and *you can make a difference.* If you believe you can do something for God, you're buying into God's view of you. Plenty of teens have already signed up and can say why they want to change their corner of the world.

- from a girl who counsels teens with life-threatening illnesses: "I got so much support when I was ill that I want to give back to the hospital and community."
- from a boy who tutors younger children: "I can show them that smart teens are cool and get them started on that path."
- from a student who is a junior counselor in city recreational programs: "I've got time. I can use it to make a difference or to get into trouble."
- from a boy who works with the Red Cross and coordinated construction of a neighborhood hockey rink: "I'm responsible to help out."
- from a girl who tutors Hispanic and Hmong adults for their citizenship examinations: "I want others to have the confidence and opportunities I have."
- from a teen who championed a day care center at her high school

for teen mothers: "I can't help helping people when the cards are stacked against them."[1]

These teens know their actions matter and know that the smiles on the faces they help signal that a whole heap of a different kind of fun is going on. They're starting to know their missions and it's shaping their plans to be teachers, attorneys, pediatricians. The specifics of their plans will change, but their goal of making a difference won't.

TIME TRUTH #3: JESUS KEPT HIS LIFE IN BALANCE.

If you sign up for God's team, that doesn't mean that you spend every spare moment being sucked dry by the needs of others. You get to enjoy God's creation, fun times with friends, learning for the heck of it, the ups and downs of families. In other words, you get a balanced life.

And Jesus modeled that life for you. When he was tired, he rested. When the crowds overwhelmed him, he left. When he received bad news, he retreated with his best friends. If Jesus had time for weddings, boat rides, visits with close friends, and his relationship with God, then so do you.

And you have to be filled up to serve. Ditch the image of servants of God who wear themselves out, neglect their families, and die of exhaustion. Jesus said he came not just so you'd have life, but abundant life—a life with plenty of resources, incredible richness (John 10:10). Not riches, but richness. You can't concentrate on the needs of others if you're forever trashed. You don't want to feel like someone else is driving your car in the race of life—and you're just along as a passenger, ready to lean out the window and heave when the car hits the curves.

So how do you create a balanced life? Accept that you're more

---

[1]"Meet 10 teen heroes." Minneapolis Star Tribune, Thursday, April 23, 1998, page E2.

than an amoeba. You're a complicated person. God expects you to take care of yourself:

- You've got a *brain* to pump up. Sure, learning gives you something to talk about besides the latest Oscar winners. (Don't say, "I'm not that good at school." Did you know that there's a link between Alzheimer's and people who stop using their brains?)
- You've got a *spirit* to nourish. God wants to pour love, joy, peace, patience, kindness, goodness, faithfulness, gentleness, and self-control into your life. (Don't say, "I'm not into spiritual growth." God wants to give you inner stuff—inward strength.)
- You've got a *body* to tend. Not just staying away from immoral sex and illegal drugs, but making exercise an immovable rock in your schedule. Find moves you like to do and do them. (Don't say, "I'm not a jock." After all, lots of former high school football heroes manage to misplace all of the habits they acquired through athletics except drinking beer.)

Look at the word "recreation" carefully. *Re*-creation. Balancing your life puts you on the path to being all you can be, allowing yourself to be zapped with God's creative powers.

Of course, at some points, balance is impossible. Finals week probably isn't the time to invest yourself in a new hobby no matter how renewing it is. And if you take a week-long missions trip, you get by without reading encyclopedias for the time you're gone. In the big scheme of life, new parents are often out of balance. Illnesses may make you pull inward. Career changes can drain your energy. But if you *never* have time to renew yourself, you're denying the way God designed you. Chances are you're a grouch.

TIME TRUTH #4:
JESUS KEPT IT SIMPLE.

Have you ever seen a movie or even a picture where Jesus or his disciples carried *anything*? Okay, so those pictures wouldn't be real.

But did they haul around a couple of tent rolls as they moved from place to place? Pack along a kettle or a couple of spoons for cooking? A change of clothes? They must have had a few things, but one of the reasons Jesus was so available to others was that he kept his life simple. He meant it when he said,

> Consider the lilies of the field, how they grow; they neither toil nor spin, yet I tell you, even Solomon in all his glory was not clothed like one of these. But if God so clothes the grass of the field, which is alive today and tomorrow is thrown into the oven, will [God] not much more clothe you—you of little faith? (Matthew 6:28–30, NRSV)

The Bible has plenty of examples of passionate disciples of Jesus who didn't sell everything, including Joseph of Arimathea (who provided the tomb where Jesus was buried) and Lydia (whose home the early Christians used as a gathering place). It isn't money but the *love* of money that's the root of all evil.

But—things complicate our lives. We own things. They also own us.

Do you have a car yet? You pay a price for the freedom wheels give you. Earning the money for insurance and gas. Time out for oil changes and engine maintenance. Hours spent waiting around the license bureau to renew tabs. From beginning to end, you have to figure out what to buy, then maintain it, repair it, and dispose of it when it breaks.

That's why lifestyle choices are so important—how much stuff you have determines how much time you have available. Want to argue that things really save you time?

■ *What about washing machines?* At the turn of the century women reported that laundry was their most time-consuming task. Today women report the same thing. What happened? Once we stopped hauling water and scraping soap to wash clothes, we changed our definition of dirt. People used to wear the same pants for at least a week even if they worked in horse barns. Now something is considered dirty if it's been in contact with human skin for more than 15 seconds.

- *Computers?* Ha! In the 1960s computers were heralded as the key to a 30-hour work week for everyone. Instead, we create more complicated but no more useful reports. We force ourselves to keep up with multiple email addresses checked several times a day.

- *Watches?* They're more convenient than carrying a clock, but as an African told a friend of ours, "You Americans have all the watches, but we have all the time."

You don't have to wear your mom's cast-off clothing or yearn for a Yugo, but look ahead to what you're committing to. Jane and Kevin both live in decent homes in the burbs, but each of our families managed to have one parent stay home with preschoolers. How? From the get-go we said no to a whopper mortgage and car payments that required a second income.

A simple lifestyle isn't like taking vows to be a monk. It's weighing the benefits you get against the time and freedom you give up.

TIME TRUTH #5:
JESUS KNEW WHAT IT
MEANT TO SHINE.

Jesus told us, "You are the light of the world. A city built on a hill cannot be hid. . . . Let your light shine before others, so that they may see your good works and give glory to your Father in heaven" (Matthew 5:14, 16, NRSV). Two thousand years later, Andy Warhol said, "In the future, everyone will be world famous for 15 minutes."

There's more than one way to shine famously, though. You can do something incredibly stupid, astoundingly evil, extraordinarily lucky, disastrously unfortunate—or astonishingly well.

Some people have two 15-minute moments of fame. First they shine, then they fall. The athletes convicted of domestic abuse. The televangelists jailed for tax evasion. The politicians shielding their faces from news cameras. And some fall, only to return to shine. The ex-addicts who use all their resources for a drop-in counseling center. The former female inmate who works to establish an education program for convicts that are mothers of young children.

Makes fame sound pretty dangerous. But there's another kind, one that's seldom on the evening news. It's subtle—even invisible. It's doing what you were meant to do, right where God wants you to do it, no matter what anyone else thinks. It's living out the words of Paul: "Do everything without complaining or arguing, so that you may become blameless and pure, children of God without fault in a crooked and depraved generation, in which you shine like stars in the universe as you hold out the word of life" (Philippians 2:14–16).

Think of people you admire. Not the ones in their 15 minutes of fame but the folks who shine for God. Do you wonder how they arrange their lives so they can shine for God?

Guess what? You have just as much time to shine for God as they do. If that's your goal, you have as many minutes in each hour, as many hours in each day. You may need more sleep or less, but over a lifetime the people who shine are those who recognize God's call and arrange their lives to answer.

You can be a guy or girl who shines. Answering God's call might put you in medical school, on a board of directors, in front of a classroom of children, at a homeless shelter—wherever God wants you to be.

You'll have goals and a purpose.

You'll know why you're doing what you're doing.

You'll define for yourself what success means and you'll have your eyes on that prize—not the world's treasures.

You'll know that there's trouble on this planet. If it comes your way, you'll figure that's life, not God's nasty anger. And you know God is with you no matter what.

You'll have located your spot in the plans of the God who is able to "keep you from falling and to present you before his glorious presence without fault and with great joy" (Jude 24).

You'll have found your fit.

WHERE TO GO FROM HERE

1. *Figure out how to make time for God.* Look back at your type pages. What's your dominant preference? Use the suggestions in the chart below and experiment with different ways people are spiritual.

Check whether you're an Extravert or an Introvert

IF YOUR DOMINANT PREFERENCE IS: SENSING

☐ **Extraverts** might get out and enjoy the wonders of God's creation. Converse with God while biking, walking, or even gazing at sunsets.

☐ **Introverts** might choose an organized prayer activity—read a daily devotional or meet with a Bible study group. You're the type who might stick to a set time each day.

IF YOUR DOMINANT PREFERENCE IS: INTUITION

☐ **Extraverts** might find a variety of ways. Place a picture or poem on your dresser and pray each time you look at it. Join a group for worship and prayer. Use poetry, art, and classes from a wide variety of perspectives to turn your thoughts to God.

☐ **Introverts** might get time alone with God. Study the Bible any way you like. And all that time you spend musing about the future and how things could be different? Make it conversation with God.

IF YOUR DOMINANT PREFERENCE IS: THINKING

☐ **Extraverts** might use time with God to search for truth. Admit your doubts to God, find others who want to debate and discuss what Jesus really meant and how it applies to today. Pray as you read the newspaper, exercise, or walk.

☐ **Introverts** might find God in solitude—either in studying all you can to define truth and your beliefs or by talking to God while you mow, rake, listen to someone, clean, or play with a person who needs your help.

IF YOUR DOMINANT PEFERENCE IS: FEELING

☐ **Extraverts** might see God in the people around you. Develop a habit to pray for them. Build some deep spiritual friendships and share how God is at work in your lives.

☐ **Introverts** might find time alone in your favorite settings, where you can appreciate God's handiwork while you pray. Read encouraging scripture passages as if they were written to you (such as Philippians 1:3–6).

2. *Get a start on your mission in life.* Check at the end of the next (and final) chapter for tips on writing your own mission statement.

3. *Keep a time journal.* You can't save or rearrange time if you don't know where you spend it. So track for a week how you use your time: school, work, friends, family time, getting close to God—whatever. School is pretty much covered, but even then tracking where and how you spend your time might be helpful. Once you've got that data, get honest with yourself about time wasters. What in your life isn't doing you or anyone else any good? And what are you doing each day for your brain, spirit, and body?

4. *Break loose.* Most of us could stand to simplify. What in your life is just clutter? Clean it out. Give the extra clothes, games, leftover toys, tapes, and CDs to people who'd really use them. What good things in your life bog you down? Are you wired to the TV, telephone, or computer? Shut them off for a while and see if you free up both time and energy. You can also take the "Deserted Island Challenge." As a teen, Kevin went on a missions trip where he could have just 32 pounds of stuff for the whole summer. That included clothes, work boots, Bible, dishes, toiletries, and the duffle to stuff it all in. Get out the family scale and figure out what you would truly need if

you were limited to what you could comfortably carry in a backpack. Then go on a camping trip and live that way for a while.

5. *Time to shine.* Get a sheet of paper and write your own eulogy—that's the time at a funeral when people get up and say nice things about the person who died. What do you want people to say about you? "He pitched a shutout in the World Series" or "She ran an ad campaign that made General Motors several billion dollars" are nice. But what about how you touched people's lives, raised a family well, or gave back to your church and community? To get perspective on what matters in the long haul of life, ask some older adults what they'd like said at their funeral (and then wish them a long and happy life!).

FIND

YOUR

FIT!

WHY DOESN'T GOD JUST HAND ME THE DIRECTIONS?

A re you wondering if finding your fit is too confusing? Worried that you might sleep the rest of your life in a drainage ditch if you come up with the "wrong" answer? Wishing life weren't so complicated or that God—or your parents or school—would just type up directions for you and put them on the back of a cereal box? Well, imagine what it might be like if someone simply *told* you how you were designed and what you should be . . .

THE RORY STORY

Rory lived in a faraway place and time where no one had to worry about what they'd be when they grew up. The government in Rory's country had invested decades of research and trillions of dollars into a vocational assessment system. All children, on their fourth birthdays, were brought to an Appraisal Center. This government-run agency had a tightly focused mission:

> To determine the true worth of each child—
> the optimum developmental course for each citizen—
> based on interests, talents, and abilities.
> An unproductive life is a misery indeed.

Now, this society was wise enough to know that it takes more than a few simple tests to perfectly identify a child's right career fit. The children spent two weeks eating, sleeping, and playing at the Center—a time filled with special treats, magic shows, incredible toys, and adventures by the minute, all carefully supervised not just by Appraisal Specialists but by interactive, kid-friendly Robotic Appraisal Playmates, affectionately known as RAPPERS. Picture a cuddly sci-fi droid.

Each child was assigned to a RAPPER, which played with the child, answered questions, helped with meals and bedtimes, and recorded each decision, emotional reaction, interaction—every move the child made during their time together. The RAPPER data was processed by the central appraisal computers. At the end of the two weeks, each child went home with a detailed report of his or her vocational aptitudes as well as school assignments, extracurricular activities, and designated core friendship circle for the next twelve years—all designed to heighten the child's essential training for the job he or she would eventually have in society.

Schools were tidy and pleasant because everyone studied things that interested them. Failure was unknown because everyone only did things they were good at. Friendships were deep because the preselected core groups had so much in common. And everyone moved through training with a satisfied security, knowing exactly what job awaited. Yes, people were happy. No one littered in the parks, buses ran on time, and life was serene.

Until Rory came along. You see, Rory's parents weren't good at tracking the calendar—especially when they were on vacation. And when Rory's fourth birthday rolled along, she was camping halfway up a mountain with her parents. Out of touch with the rest of the world. Out of reach of the Appraisal Center Specialists. Out of luck for being appraised.

When her parents presented Rory a few weeks later, the Appraisal Center Specialists huffed and threw up their hands. "We're afraid we can't tell you what your daughter should be," they said. "She missed her appointment. Our tests are calibrated for children who are four years old—not four years and four weeks. And we're full up. We're sorry, but perhaps you'll be more careful with your next child."

Plugging their ears to the dire warning that Rory would be a misfit, a welfare case for life because she lacked Appraisal Center guidance, her parents devised their own plan. "We'll see what she likes to do. And find teachers who won't laugh if she struggles. Take her to different environments so she can see what they're like. Let her find friends from different core groups and try different hobbies."

And that's what they did. At first their neighbors were shocked. Businesses they visited where aghast. Teachers were puzzled with what to do with her. But once everyone got used to having Rory on the prowl, people became curious, then envious, of her chance to explore.

All the other children were expected to like each class and activity on their list. Rory got to say, "*Blechh*. I want to do something else."

Other children all did well at everything—everything they were allowed to try, anyway. Rory had to work absurdly hard at some of her classes. When one of her friends said she felt sorry Rory took so long to finish some science class experiments, Rory said, "Well, maybe I'm not going to be a physicist, but it felt really good when my answers finally made sense. That made it fun."

Rory had lots of fun. Since her twelve-year schedule wasn't set, she had time for art classes. Automaton design. Analyzing mythical beasts and their figurative use in modern-day business management. She stuck with sports because they were interesting, even if she couldn't win ribbons or trophies. She went on different kinds of adventures with different friends. Climbed trees *and* played flute. Joined the debate team *and* took statistics for the heck of it.

And eventually, Rory found lots of things she liked to do. She planned to weave the ones she liked the most into her career goals and keep the rest for Saturdays.

And on her little sister's fourth birthday, Rory's whole family just happened to be on a river raft, out of touch again—along with three other families whose children just turned four. Whose parents had never been camping—not a designated activity—and thought it might be a wild challenge.

And everyone wondered if perhaps Rory wasn't the luckiest girl in the land.

WHAT'S OUR WEIRD POINT?

So what? What's our point? Well, God could tell you exactly what to do. Maybe right now that even sounds good—a burning bush that shouts, "Apply for a scholarship to Oxfoooord. Major in cake decoratinnnng. Buy sixteen shares of Amazon-dot-commmmmm. . . ." And off you'd go, no litter in the parks or anything. You'd be so well heeled you'd never leave your gum under a school bus seat or spit anywhere but a sink or a dentist's office.

But then you'd be like all the RAPPER-diagnosed kids in Rory's country. You'd be *told* exactly what to do. (Think about that. Isn't that exactly what you like best about your life today—when people tell you what to do? Highly doubtful.) You'd even be told what you could *try*.

And that's why the people around Rory felt they'd missed something. They saw that uncertainty and failure aren't the worst that can happen. The "confusion" and "problems" the Appraisal Centers helped them avoid are some of life's gigantic blessings. Rory experienced all kinds of things that were out of their reach:

RORY GOT TO EXPLORE.

The riot of discovery is a highlight of being human. You may not trek to the other side of the globe, but you can explore *you* and how you fit in an ever-widening world all around you. It's a frontier no one else can explore. Yes, we can give you quizzes and people can tell you what they observe, but only you can put all of the pieces together—after all, only you have any experience being you!

And does it really matter that you miss some moves while you're checking out who you are? Just remember, Columbus was on his way to India when he bumped into America. Accidental detours are sometimes fantastic exploits full of crazy friendships and priceless discoveries—even if you just find out what it takes to do another person's job.

RORY GOT TO CHOOSE.

We're wired to want to make our own choices—the whole free-will thing. As parents, Kevin and Jane know that if you really want a two-year-old to put on shoes, you say, "Would you like to wear your tennies or sandals?" so she thinks she has a choice. Not, "Put on your shoes right now!" (at least not the first time). And even as adults, people want a say in what happens to them.

Many of the adults who take LifeKeys, the course *Find Your Fit* is based on, tell us things like

- "My parents said they wouldn't pay for college unless I became a doctor."
- "I had no choice but to take over the family business."
- "I didn't choose a career—everyone said I'd just marry and have babies anyway."

Sometimes as these people rechoose a career through *LifeKeys*, they discover that the way they were funneled actually does suit them. Sometimes they opt for a change. But by making their own choices—finding their fit based on God, not others—they buy into their future.

RORY GOT TO STRUGGLE.

Maybe it sounds like a relief to only take classes you're good at. But be honest—haven't you had a toughie class turn into a winner because of the zany teacher? Or where you bonded with a new friend who helped you through the homework? Or when you finally earned a good grade because of hair-pulling, late-evening, determined hard work—and you felt like a billion bucks? Some of life's best things come only through struggle.

RORY GOT TO CHOOSE HER FRIENDS.

Sure, sometimes you wish your whole crew wanted to see the same movie, but disagreements and discussions and opinions are what life is all about. Not to mention that with a variety of friends you get to try rock climbing or impressionist painting or making sushi just because someone else knows all about it.

RORY GOT TO FAIL.

What's so hot about failure? Provided no one's laughing at you, failure is a God-given chance to grow patience and self-control. And failing as a kid is the best preparation for being a grown-up who can say things like, "I made a mistake. I'm sorry." Besides, when your first failures are at something little—like finding out you're best built to play drums, not clarinet—it cuts the dread out of trying new things. You learn that no one's good at everything.

RORY GOT TO DECIDE WHO SHE WAS.

She got to test the theory that God designed her for a great, unique, fulfilling life. And she found out for herself that God keeps promises. That she had a future.

If you're trying to do what God has in mind, even detours can turn out to be just what you need to make the most of your future. Jane started out as a bank examiner—*not* a good fit for her personality type (INFJ). But she met great people, learned about business, completed an MBA, did lots of writing, and meandered to being a controller, a consultant, and finally a writer—on subjects as far removed from finance as possible. Jane's journey wasn't a straight line from *A* to *B*, but as she looks back, each detour gave to her valuable experiences and wisdom.

By the time he was in high school, Kevin knew he wanted to be in full-time ministry, but he didn't know where. He flip-flopped through a variety of majors—from plant science to Mandarin Chinese to teaching—until he landed in courses heavy in writing. As he trained in graduate school, he discovered he liked working with youth and was able to pastor a large youth group for more than five years. He couldn't have planned to be in the writing and editing ministry he's in now because jobs are so rare. But when he received an invitation to work in Christian publishing, he knew it tied together everything he'd done with his life so far.

And we're both still young. Shocked we're already on second careers? We aren't surprised at all—most people now go through around seven. Seven *careers*, not seven jobs. But we aren't hung up about our futures. Why?

We've found our fit.

We know what we do well.

We've got a handle on our values.

We've practiced choosing between right and right in the world of work and are still on course.

And most important, we've got a few years under our belts. We can look back and see how God guided all our planning and decision-making and shot-in-the-dark choices and even misguided choices. We know we can trust God.

Now it's *your* chance to get started on the path that will build your trust in God. It's the path that fits you best. But there isn't just one right fit. You may find two or three in your lifetime.

And you won't figure out your fit in just a quick flip through this book. It may take weeks, months, or even years, depending on where you started—because in order to *Find Your Fit*, you have to be able to say some things like you mean it:

- "I'm made in God's image." Can you say that? And believe what it implies—that you are valuable just as you are because God created you uniquely?
- "God gave me a special blend of life gifts, spiritual gifts, personality type, and values. I'm fearfully and wonderfully made." Are

you convinced that God gave you just the right gifts for who you are?

■ "God has plans for me, to flourish and do good works." Are you going to keep searching out how God wants you to passionately use your talents and gifts?

However you fit into God's plan, rest assured it's a *perfect* fit. Not a hand-me-down slot, but a place where you can

do what you do best

revel in being part of something huger than yourself

know God

be different

and make a difference.

WHERE DO YOU GO FROM HERE?

1. *Fill in the blanks.* Have you completed "All About Me" on page 207? Right now you probably feel like you have a couple of the pieces nailed—maybe you're really sure of your spiritual gifts and values. But if you're like most people, you're still searching in some other areas. Choose the area you want to "finish" next—life gifts, spiritual gifts, personality, values, passions. Go back to that chapter and look through "Where Do You Go From Here?" Pick out something to do and set a goal. What will you do this week to find out more? This month? This evening?

2. *Find a "Find Your Fit" Partner.* Finding your fit is a big job. You can do some of it by yourself, but the best decisions and insights involve your head tangled together with other people's brains. A partner can keep you motivated and moving. Some suggested partners:

■ *Your parents.* Make sure they read our introduction. They've been there, done that as far as deciding careers. And they've already got a lot invested in your future. They can set you up to

interview people they know in a variety of jobs, share their insights about your gifts and personality, and add realism about
college funds and vo-tech options.

■ *Your friends.* They're in the same boat and on a similar timeline.
See if your youth pastor might get some *Find Your Fit* small
groups started or start your own. Meet regularly, set goals from
our suggestions, and report to each other on the progress you're
making. Above all, encourage each other.

■ *Adult mentors.* Lots of adults willingly lend a helping hand to
teens who want to scour their brains. Ask your parents who they
know. See if your favorite teacher might be willing to meet with
you once a month. Or check with aunts, uncles, even older siblings.

3. *Write down what adds up to you.* Get a notebook to jot ran-
domly the facts you know about you. Things like

■ My biggest motivator is knowing that my efforts will directly help
someone else.

■ While I hope to find a college that has a strong business department, a track team I can join, and that's in a small town, the location's probably least important to me.

■ I still don't know what I want to be, but I want a job where I
can work with computers at a company that will help pay for
more training.

■ I want to teach art, but those jobs are scarce. If I can't do it as a
profession, I could volunteer at a museum, use my gifts at
church, etc.

■ I want to avoid careers that make it tough to take time out for
being an at-home parent.

4. *Define a meaningful life.* Adults call it "writing a mission statement." While you may not be ready to set your mission for life,
you've already got a great start on your "How You Fit Together"
page. In the same place you wrote answers to number 3 above, set

up a doodle page for your mission. Divide the page into three sections. Label the first section "What I'm great at" and list the life gifts and spiritual gifts you most want to use right now. Label the next section "What I need to do my best" and look at your personality type and values to fill this in. Write down stuff like "My work environment needs to include friendships" or "I work best at odd hours—what careers won't lock me into 9 to 5?" Label the third section, "Why I'm here." Doodle about what role you want to play in community—either the world right around you or the big community of planet Earth. This may echo your job—being an environmental engineer, a social worker, a teacher, a minister. Or it might echo a lifelong cause—planting trees, influencing government, befriending shut-ins.

Mission statements aren't hard to come up with. They don't have to be flowery and frameable. Just wrap together your doodles and state what you want to do with your life. Briefly. So you can remember it. And go for it.

ALL ABOUT ME

I have identified the following talents:

I believe I have the following spiritual gifts:

With my personality preferences for _____ _____ _____ _____ these things are important as I choose places to put my gifts to use:

My top eight values are:

My passions tell me I can make a difference in my world in these ways:

VALUES

- Accuracy
- Achievement
- Advancement
- Adventure
- Aesthetics
- Artistic expression
- Authenticity
- Balance
- Challenge
- Competency
- Competition
- Conformity
- Contribution
- Control
- Cooperation
- Creativity
- Efficiency
- Fairness
- Family
- Financial security
- Flexibility
- Friendship
- Generosity
- Happiness
- Humor
- Independence
- Influence
- Integrity
- Learning
- Leisure
- Location
- Love
- Loyalty
- Nature
- Organization
- Peace
- Perseverance
- Personal development
- Physical fitness & health
- Power
- Prestige
- Purity
- Recognition
- Relationship with God
- Responsibility
- Security
- Self-Respect
- Service
- Stability
- Tolerance
- Tradition
- Variety